Lowfat Beef

Also by
Jackie Eddy and Eleanor Clark

Absolute Beginner's Cookbook
Absolute Beginner's Cookbook 2
Lowfat Gourmet Chicken

Lowfat Beef

Jackie Eddy
and
Eleanor Clark

PRIMA PUBLISHING

PRIMA PUBLISHING and colophon are registered trademarks of Prima Communications, Inc.

On the cover: Trevor's New York Strip Loin Steaks with Three-Peppercorn Sauce (page 88)

Library of Congress Cataloging-in-Publication Data
Eddy, Jackie.
    Lowfat beef / by Jackie Eddy & Eleanor Clark.
      p.   cm.
    Includes index.
    ISBN 0-7615-0191-6
    1. Low-fat diet—Recipes.   2. Cookery (Beef).   I. Clark, Eleanor.
II. Title.
RM237.7.E437   1996
641.6'62—dc20   96-18472
                                                          CIP

96 97 98 99 00 AA 10 9 8 7 6 5 4 3 2 1
Printed in the United States of America

A Note on Nutritional Data:
A per-serving nutritional breakdown of each recipe is given rounded to the nearest whole number. If a range is given for an ingredient amount, the breakdown is based on the smaller number. If a range is given for the serving size, the breakdown is based on the larger number. If a choice of ingredients is given in an ingredient listing, the breakdown is calculated using the first choice. "Optional" ingredients or those for which no specific amount is stated are not included in the breakdown. Nutritional content may vary depending on the specific brands or types of ingredients used. The nutritional information for beef was supplied by the U.S. Department of Agriculture.

How to Order:
Single copies may be ordered from Prima Publishing, P.O. Box 1260BK, Rocklin, CA 95677; telephone (916) 632-4400. Quantity discounts are also available. On your letterhead, include information concerning the intended use of the books and the number of books you wish to purchase.

Visit us online at http://www.primapublishing.com

To David Brown
(Brother and Friend)

Contents

Preface

My brother David on a recent visit said, "You know Jackie, you and Eleanor were never slimmer than when you were working on the *Lowfat Gourmet Chicken* cookbook." So when our publisher called and asked if we would like to do a lowfat beef cookbook, it didn't take too long for us to decide.

The object of this book is to offer a wide range of beef dishes that are low in fat and, in many cases, reduced in salt, without sacrificing taste.

We have included a good selection of fiber-rich dishes as well. Studies have shown that fiber helps to prevent the absorption of a small amount of our fat intake and may also help to protect against cancer of the stomach and colon. It is encouraging to see so many young people adopting healthier choices in their eating habits. It wasn't too long ago that only people with heart disease embarked on a diet and only after they had suffered a heart attack or stroke.

Many individuals concerned with weight-loss now count grams of fat rather than calories as in the past. There are three types of fats in the foods we eat: saturated (the ones that normally stay hard at room temperature and the ones we want to avoid); polyunsaturated fats; and monounsaturated fats (these stay liquid at room temperature). The latter two are found in oils made from sunflowers, safflowers, canola, corn, and olives. The best way to determine the amounts of saturated, polyunsaturated, and monounsaturated fats in products is to read the nutritional information on the label. (This is usually in very fine print, so if you are our age, you will need your glasses!)

You will find that we have used soy sauce in many of our recipes, as soy sauce has only about one-seventh the sodium content of salt. As well, we have made good use of herbs and spices to add flavor to dishes where salt has been used sparingly. Stock up on these essential flavoring agents, especially the ones you will find throughout this book. We find them the most compatible with beef.

A serving of lean beef is not only a good source or iron, it also provides you with more than 25 percent of your daily requirement of five essential nutrients: protein, niacin, zinc, and vitamins B6 and B12. These are essential for growth and development as well as energy and metabolism.

The whole country seems to be in pursuit of health, wealth, and a lowfat diet. And for those who love their beef, this book—with its wide selection of recipes to choose from—should be a solution.

—Jackie Eddy

Acknowledgments

We would like to thank the many friends and relatives who gave their valuable input. Your enthusiastic support and interest makes each book we undertake so much more enjoyable.

A special mention to: Leslie Caithness, Mary Collister (you are always there for us Mary), Larry and Ann Margared Eddy-Silva, Bill and Jaime Clark, Sheilah Montgomery, Maria Ventura-Silva, Betty Jean Baldwin, Bill and Judy Trowbridge, Brent and Louise Lalonde, Sheri Sept (our leftover lunchtime tester), Jane Liden, Shawn Caithness, Marlene Harms, Kathy Clark, Bella Marcovitch, Mary Kling, and Kathy Keeler at the Calgary Beef Information Centre.

A special thanks to our husbands—to Trevor for some great ideas and to Don for a great appetite and some challenging bridge games at our weekly "beef and bridge" testings.

Lowfat Beef

Appetizers

A ppetizers made with beef may seem like overkill if you are serving beef as an entrée, but they are ideal if you are looking for a substantial hors d'oeuvre to take to a potluck dinner or if you want a healthy appetizer to serve with a meatless main course that may not contain enough protein. Offer any one of these toothsome appetizers with a pre-dinner drink and show your friends they are special and cared for.

Teriyaki Beef on Skewers

You can serve these hot as appetizers, as a main course, or cold for picnics. We took some of these on a picnic in the summer, and they were a huge success!

Makes 8 to 10 servings

1	pound lean sirloin steak, partially frozen
1/4	cup lite soy sauce
1	tablespoon sherry
2	teaspoons sesame oil
3	to 4 cloves garlic, minced
1	tablespoon honey
1	teaspoon grated fresh ginger

Cut partially frozen beef into strips, on an angle, making sure to remove all visible fat.

Combine soy sauce, sherry, sesame oil, garlic, honey, and ginger. Add strips to marinade and transfer to plastic bag or container. Marinate for 2 to 4 hours. Drain and reserve marinade.

Thread strips onto skewers. (If using wooden skewers, be sure to soak them in hot water for at least 1 hour prior to use.) Barbecue or broil for roughly 4 minutes on each side over medium heat, brushing with reserved marinade.

Each serving provides:

90	Calories	1 g	Carbohydrate
12 g	Protein	146 mg	Sodium
4 g	Total fat	34 mg	Cholesterol

Steak Tartare

This appetizer has been around for quite a long time. It was very popular in the early sixties and now seems to be back in vogue—perhaps because it is full of protein and low in fat. (The first time Eleanor ordered this in a restaurant, the waiter asked whether she would like it rare, medium, or well-done!)

Make sure you use only the choicest, freshest meat. It is best if you chop the steak yourself, making sure it is free of all fat and gristle. Use the same day as purchased and chop as close to serving time as possible—ideally, within the hour of serving to ensure the freshness and flavor of the dish. Use immaculately clean knives and chopping board. (If you don't have proper knives or the inclination to chop it yourself, see Leslie's Steak Tartare recipe next.)

Unfortunately, there is an ever-growing concern about the threat of harmful bacteria in raw meat. It is advised that raw meat not be served to the elderly, the young, or those with a compromised immune system. Always buy your meat from a trusted purveyor, use only one cutting board for raw meats and a separate one for vegetables, and carefully and thoroughly scrub everything that comes into contact with the meat with hot, soapy water.

Makes 4 to 6 servings

8	ounces fresh beef tenderloin, finely ground (see note)
1/2	teaspoon salt
2	teaspoons dry mustard
1	tablespoon grated onion
1	tablespoon finely chopped green onion
1/4	cup minced fresh parsley
1 1/2	teaspoons Worcestershire sauce
1	teaspoon freshly ground black pepper
1/8	teaspoon paprika
3	tablespoons tiny capers, drained
1	loaf cocktail rye bread, thinly sliced

Thoroughly blend the beef, salt, mustard, onion, green onion, parsley, Worcestershire sauce, and black pepper using the hand and fingers to squeeze. Refrigerate a couple of hours before serving. To serve, mound on a platter, sprinkle with paprika, and garnish with capers, or have a bowl of drained capers beside the seasoned ground meat.

Serve with rye bread and have a pepper grinder handy. Guests will spread beef on the bread and sprinkle a few capers on top.

Note: To finely grind the beef, put it through the meat grinder twice. If you have no grinder, use two French chopping knives and chop meat, rotating chopping board slowly and making sure meat is minced finely.

Each serving provides:			
204	Calories	29 g	Carbohydrate
13 g	Protein	654 mg	Sodium
4 g	Total fat	24 mg	Cholesterol

Leslie's Steak Tartare

From a darling daughter-in-law comes this faster and more economical version of steak tartare. Leslie is a terrific cook who believes in exposing her children to sophisticated food—an important social education. On special occasions, they have had this dish as a meal, accompanied by a salad. Make sure you use the freshest top-quality meat and prepare it close to serving time.

Leslie claims that the HP sauce is the "secret" ingredient to this dish. HP sauce is a steak sauce available in most markets; A1 steak sauce is a good substitute. For the bread garnish, Leslie uses a fresh baguette, sliced and brushed with olive oil, dusted with garlic salt, and broiled—like crostini.

Due to the threat of harmful bacteria in raw meat, it is advised that it not be served to the elderly, the young, or those with a compromised immune system. Always buy your meat from a trusted purveyor, use only one cutting board for raw meats and a separate one for vegetables, and carefully and thoroughly scrub everything that comes into contact with the raw meat with hot, soapy water.

Makes 8 to 12 servings

Steak

1	pound top sirloin or top round, trimmed of all visible fat, gristle, or sinew, cut into 1¹/₂-inch squares
¹/₄	cup finely minced yellow onion
2	tablespoons chopped fresh Italian parsley
1¹/₂	tablespoons HP sauce
1	uncooked egg yolk
1	teaspoon salt
	freshly ground black pepper, to taste
¹/₂	teaspoon Worcestershire sauce

Garnish

3	to 4 Bibb or Red Leaf lettuce leaves
¹/₃	cup snipped chives
1	small red onion, very finely sliced
4	tablespoons tiny capers, drained
2	to 3 sun-dried tomatoes, reconstituted (see note)
1	loaf cocktail rye or black bread, sliced

Combine all of the steak tartare ingredients in a bowl. Place half of the mixture in a food processor and pulse on and off for about 8 seconds or until desired texture is reached. Be careful not to overprocess. The mixture can either be quite smooth or more "chunky," depending on your preference. Process the other half to the same consistency. Refrigerate until serving time.

Arrange on a large round plate lined with lettuce. Place meat in center in ring form or in a small round bowl. Sprinkle all garnishes around and on top of meat. Serve bread on the side.

Note: To reconstitute sun-dried tomatoes, place tomatoes in boiling water and cook over high heat for two minutes. Drain and use as directed.

Each serving provides:

179	Calories	16 g	Carbohydrate
10 g	Protein	456 mg	Sodium
8 g	Total fat	43 mg	Cholesterol

Stuffed Mushroom Caps

These may be made an hour or two ahead of time and refrigerated until baking time.

Makes 6 servings

18	to 24 large mushrooms
2	teaspoons canola oil or safflower oil
4	tablespoons finely chopped green onion (include some green)
1/4	cup grated raw mushrooms (you can use some of the stems)
1/2	pound extra-lean ground beef
1/4	cup salsa
	celery salt, to taste
1/4	cup fresh whole wheat bread crumbs

Preheat oven to 400°. Wipe mushroom caps (never wash them, because they retain too much moisture). Remove stems and place caps, cavity side up, on a baking sheet sprayed with nonstick cooking spray.

In a small nonstick skillet, heat oil and sauté green onion until soft; add grated mushrooms and beef. Cook over medium heat until all traces of pink disappear from the meat. There will be some juice in the pan, but it will be juice from the mushrooms, not fat (if you have used extra-lean beef). Add salsa. Continue to cook until most of the liquid has evaporated. Remove from heat and stir in celery salt and bread crumbs. Let cool.

Fill mushroom caps, mounding the filling slightly. Bake for about 10 minutes. Serve hot.

Each serving provides:

126	Calories		4 g	Carbohydrate
9 g	Protein		51 mg	Sodium
8 g	Total fat		26 mg	Cholesterol

Mexican Half Hats

These are a nice spicy treat nestled in a bread casing. They freeze well, but you should freeze them after baking.

Makes 20

1/4	pound extra-lean ground beef
1/3	cup salsa
1/4	teaspoon pepper
1	loaf frozen bread dough, thawed
2	to 3 tablespoons skim milk

Cook ground beef in a small frying pan over medium heat. When almost cooked through, stir in salsa and pepper. Cook for 2 more minutes. Remove from heat and let cool.

Preheat oven to 350°. Roll out the dough and cut into circles with a 3-inch cookie cutter. Place a teaspoon of filling in the middle, moisten edges of dough with skim milk and fold in half, pressing edges together and crimping with a fork. Spray a cookie sheet with nonstick cooking spray. Place the pieces on the cooking sheet and let rise for about 30 minutes.

Bake for 15 minutes or until golden brown on top. Serve hot with extra salsa for dipping.

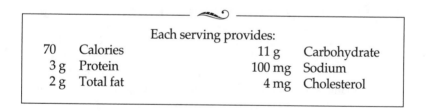

Each serving provides:

70	Calories	11 g	Carbohydrate
3 g	Protein	100 mg	Sodium
2 g	Total fat	4 mg	Cholesterol

Ground Beef Tartlets

This recipe calls for filo pastry, which is relatively low in fat and—once you get the hang of it—a snap to use. For handling filo dough, read the instructions on the package in addition to our directions. Unused filo will keep for two weeks in the refrigerator.

The tartlet shells can be frozen after baking and will last up to four weeks. If you plan to freeze the tartlets, do not put the topping on until the day you serve them.

Makes 34 to 36 tarts

Tartlets

6	sheets filo dough
1/2	pound extra-lean ground beef
1	small onion, finely minced
1/4	cup flour
1	teaspoon Worcestershire sauce
3/4	teaspoon salt
	dash of pepper
1	egg
1/2	cup 2 percent evaporated canned milk

Topping

1/4	cup lowfat mayonnaise
1/4	cup grated Parmesan cheese, fresh or packaged

Preheat oven to 425°. Spread 1 sheet of filo dough on the working surface and spray lightly with nonstick cooking spray. Top with a second sheet of filo and spray; repeat a third time. Using a sharp knife, cut the filo into squares, roughly 3 inches, and gently mold the squares into 1 3/4-inch muffin tins, with a 1/2-inch overhang to create a tulip-like effect. Repeat process with remaining three sheets of filo.

Combine ground beef, onion, flour, Worcestershire sauce, salt, pepper, and egg in a food processor and blend. Add milk and blend until smooth and paste-like. (If you don't have a food processor, use a mixer: combine first 7 ingredients, then add the milk a little at a time.)

Place 1 teaspoon of the filling into the unbaked tart shells and bake for 15 minutes or until the pastry is golden-brown.

While the pastry is in the oven, make the topping by combining the mayonnaise with the Parmesan cheese.

Remove the pastries from the oven and put a dollop of the topping on each tart and return to the oven for an additional 5 minutes. Serve hot.

Each serving provides:			
44	Calories	3 g	Carbohydrate
2 g	Protein	95 mg	Sodium
2 g	Total fat	13 mg	Cholesterol

Samosas

Like the previous recipe, samosas use filo pastry. Or, the pastry for Empanadas may be used in this recipe, if you prefer.

The triangles may be frozen unbaked. Freeze overnight on the baking sheet and then transfer to a freezer bag. Use a straw to suck out as much air as possible from the freezer bag, thus creating a vacuum seal. Bake directly from the freezer.

Makes 3^1/$_2$ to 4 dozen

1	tablespoon olive oil
1	tablespoon butter or margarine
1	large onion, finely chopped
2	cloves garlic, minced
1	pound extra-lean ground beef
1	teaspoon coriander
^{1}/$_2$	teaspoon salt
^{1}/$_4$	teaspoon pepper
1	teaspoon curry powder
^{1}/$_2$	teaspoon cumin
1	teaspoon dried crushed red pepper (see note)
^{1}/$_2$	cup non-fat sour cream
6	sheets filo pastry

Preheat oven to 400°. Heat the oil and butter in a nonstick skillet over medium heat, and sauté the onion and garlic for 3 minutes. Add the ground beef and cook until no sign of pink remains. Add the spices and ^{1}/$_2$ cup water and cook until the moisture is absorbed. Remove from heat and stir in the sour cream. Cool.

Remove filo pastry from package and keep covered with a lightly dampened towel to prevent it from drying out. Spray 1 sheet with nonstick cooking spray; fold in half and cut into 8 strips that are 2 inches wide.

Place roughly 1 teaspoon of the filling on the bottom end of each strip. Fold the filo strip over the filling so the bottom edge meets the left edge, forming a triangle. Continue folding at right angles, tucking in any remaining filo at the end, to form the triangle-shaped samosa.

Repeat with remaining filo and filling. Spray baking sheet with nonstick cooking spray. Place triangles on baking sheet, spray them lightly with more nonstick cooking spray, and bake until golden-brown, about 12 to 15 minutes.

Note: The samosas are fairly spicy. You can cut down on the crushed red pepper (or increase it if you like a three-alarm fire going off in your mouth!).

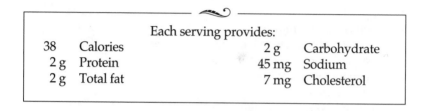

Each serving provides:			
38	Calories	2 g	Carbohydrate
2 g	Protein	45 mg	Sodium
2 g	Total fat	7 mg	Cholesterol

Empanadas

Empanadas are popular pastry turnovers found all over Latin America. They can be made ahead and frozen unbaked, or they can be baked up to one week in advance, wrapped tightly, and frozen (reheat in a preheated 400° oven for about 8 minutes before serving). Filo pastry may be used instead of the lowfat pastry.

Makes 3 dozen

Filling
2	cloves garlic, minced
1	green pepper, seeded and finely chopped
1	pound lean ground round steak
$1/2$	cup tomato paste or purée
$1/2$	teaspoon salt
3	tablespoons dry red wine
2	tablespoons capers
2	tablespoons diced olives
3	teaspoons chili powder
$1/4$	teaspoon Tabasco

Lowfat Pastry
2	cups flour
$1/4$	teaspoon salt
1	tablespoon butter or margarine
2	tablespoons non-fat sour cream

Preheat oven to 425°. Spray a nonstick skillet with nonstick cooking spray, and sauté the garlic, pepper, and beef over medium heat until no pink remains in the beef. Add the tomato paste, salt, and wine. Let cook until the liquid evaporates. Add the capers, olives, chili powder, and Tabasco. Remove from heat and let cool.

For the pastry, combine the flour, salt, butter, sour cream, and about $1/2$ cup cold water. The dough should be slightly softer than a pie crust dough. Knead well. Roll out dough and cut into circles 2 to 3 inches in diameter.

Place a spoonful of the filling into the center of each circle and fold over. Press edges together with a fork to seal. Place the empanadas on a cookie sheet and bake for 15 to 20 minutes or until golden brown.

Each serving provides:

70	Calories	7 g	Carbohydrate
3 g	Protein	108 mg	Sodium
3 g	Total fat	11 mg	Cholesterol

Soups

Soup of the evening, beautiful Soup!" sang the Mock Turtle in *Alice's Adventures in Wonderland*. It's unlikely he was singing about something poured from a can! Only long-simmering, brimming with flavor, and filled-with-goodness soups, such as you will find in this section, could induce a turtle to burst into song. You'll find that most of our soups are meals in themselves, needing nothing more than a loaf of good bread as an accompaniment.

Making soups gives the cook an opportunity to be creative, particularly when it comes time to deal with some tasty leftovers, and nearly every culture and region has created a soup from familiar ingredients. The Italians have minestrone, the Spanish have gazpacho, the Greeks have avgolemono, the French make wonderful baked onion and cheese soup, the middle Europeans are famous for borscht, the Chinese enjoy won ton soup, Canadians claim split pea soup as their own, and what would the state of our health be without that Jewish cure-all—chicken soup!

Here are a few tips on making soup:

- Celery leaves, dried in a very slow oven (200°), are a good flavoring agent for soups and stews. Crumble the dry leaves when they are cool and store them in a jar.
- If you grate your own Parmesan cheese (freshly grated is more flavorful), you will be left with part of the rind that is too hard to grate—don't throw it out! When added to the soup pot, it will add richness and flavor.
- Don't let your soups boil. A long, gentle simmer will produce a better result.
- Most soups improve with age and can be made a day or two ahead. This will allow any residual fat to rise to the top and solidify when soup is chilled, which can then be easily removed with a flat spoon.
- Soups freeze well and may be stored up to five months in the freezer.

Beef Stock

The advantage of making your own stock is being able to control the salt content. It is also economical, and once you start making your own stock, you'll also enjoy the satisfaction derived from this exercise.

Makes 10 to 12 cups

5	pounds beef bones, cut into 3-inch to 4-inch pieces (your butcher will do this for you)
2	carrots, cut in half
2	to 3 onions, skins on, cut in half
2	celery stalks, cut into 2-inch to 3-inch pieces
5	sprigs of parsley
1	bay leaf
6	black peppercorns

Preheat oven to 425°. Place bones in a large roasting pan and bake for 1 1/2 hours, turning halfway through cooking time. Add carrots to roasting pan, turn bones again, and continue to bake for an additional 30 minutes.

Remove bones and add with carrots to a large stockpot. Discard fat from roasting pan, then add water to pan and scrape up the browned bits from the bottom of the pan. Pour this water into the stockpot and add additional water to cover the bones. Add the onions, celery, parsley, bay leaf, and peppercorns. Bring to a boil over high heat, then reduce heat and simmer gently, uncovered, for 4 hours, skimming any scum that appears on the surface.

Remove from heat, strain, and discard the solids. Cover and refrigerate stock until any fat congeals on the surface. Remove fat layer. Refrigerate for up to 2 days or freeze in containers. Stock lasts up to 4 weeks when frozen. It's best to measure before you freeze so that you can defrost required amounts.

Each serving provides:			
17	Calories	1 g	Carbohydrate
2 g	Protein	18 mg	Sodium
1 g	Total fat	5 mg	Cholesterol

Beef Stock (Microwave)

Makes 4 cups

4	pounds beef bones, cut into 3-inch to 4-inch pieces (your butcher will do this for you)
1	medium carrot, sliced
1	medium onion, chopped
1	stalk celery with leaves, chopped
2	bay leaves
2	tablespoons tomato paste
$1/2$	teaspoon salt
6	black peppercorns
$1/2$	teaspoon thyme
2	beef bouillon cubes

Boil 4 cups of water, and combine with all of the ingredients in a deep, covered casserole. Microwave on high for 20 minutes. Let stand, covered, for 1 hour. Strain and discard solids. Cover and refrigerate stock until any fat congeals on the surface. Remove fat layer and store stock in refrigerator for up to 2 days or freeze.

Each serving provides:

20	Calories	2 g	Carbohydrate
2 g	Protein	716 mg	Sodium
1 g	Total fat	5 mg	Cholesterol

Spicy Steak and Kidney Bean Soup

You can use leftover steak for this recipe, or you can leave the meat out entirely and still have a very interesting and nourishing soup. Cayenne pepper is being touted as "heart friendly," so start experimenting a little. It works very well in this soup.

Makes 8 servings

1	pound small kidney beans
2	tablespoons olive oil
1	small steak, diced and trimmed of fat
1	large onion, chopped
2	medium carrots, peeled and chopped
1	large stalk celery, chopped
3	large cloves garlic, minced
1	teaspoon cumin
$1/2$	teaspoon black pepper
$1/2$	teaspoon cayenne pepper
$1/2$	cup chili sauce
10	cups homemade beef broth, or 3 cans (10 ounces each) beef broth mixed with $4^1/2$ cans water
1	can (19 ounces) tomato juice

Soak beans overnight (or see the note below to quick-soak dried beans).

Heat oil in bottom of large pot or Dutch oven. Add steak and cook until light brown. Add chopped vegetables, cover pot, and cook over medium heat for about 10 minutes, stirring occasionally.

Drain beans and add to vegetable and beef mixture. Add the spices, chili sauce, beef broth, and tomato juice. Bring to a boil. Reduce to simmer and let cook, covered, for 3 to 4 hours or until beans are tender.

Note: To quick-soak dried beans, pick over and rinse dried beans and place in a large saucepan with triple their volume of cold water. Bring water to a boil and cook beans, uncovered, over medium heat for 2 minutes. Remove pan from heat and let beans soak for 1 hour.

	Each serving provides:		
357	Calories	49 g	Carbohydrate
22 g	Protein	527 mg	Sodium
9 g	Total fat	23 mg	Cholesterol

Beef 'n Barley Soup

Makes 8 to 10 servings

1¹/₄	pounds lean ground beef
1	large onion, chopped
1	can (28 ounces) diced tomatoes
3	cans (10 ounces each) beef broth mixed with 2¹/₂ cups water
1	can (10 ounces) tomato soup, undiluted
4	medium to large carrots, finely chopped
4	large stalks celery, finely chopped
1	medium parsnip (use a vegetable peeler to peel shreds into pot)
¹/₄	cup chopped fresh parsley
¹/₂	teaspoon thyme
¹/₂	teaspoon chili powder
¹/₂	teaspoon sugar
¹/₄	teaspoon black pepper
¹/₂	cup barley

Brown ground beef and onion over moderately high heat. (If you have used regular ground beef, drain off any accumulated fat at this point.) Add all remaining ingredients and simmer, covered, for 2 to 3 hours.

Each serving provides:

245	Calories	24 g	Carbohydrate
17 g	Protein	646 mg	Sodium
10 g	Total fat	46 mg	Cholesterol

Goulash Soup

All of the ingredients come together for a soul-satisfying meal.

Makes 8 to 10 servings

1¹/₂	pounds lean beef, trimmed of all fat and cut into ¹/₂-inch cubes
1	large onion, chopped
3	cloves garlic, minced
¹/₄	teaspoon caraway seeds
2	tablespoons paprika
3	tablespoons liquid Bovril
3	tablespoons tomato paste
1	bay leaf
1	tablespoon Worcestershire sauce
¹/₂	teaspoon basil
¹/₄	teaspoon freshly ground black pepper
1	cup dried peas, washed and drained (see note)
3	cups thinly sliced carrots
3	cups cubed potatoes
¹/₂	small cabbage, shredded
¹/₃	cup minced fresh parsley

Spray bottom of large soup pot or Dutch oven with nonstick cooking spray and brown beef cubes over medium-high heat for 4 to 5 minutes. Add onion and garlic and continue to cook until onion is soft.

Sprinkle caraway seeds and paprika over mixture and continue to cook, stirring frequently, until paprika is well absorbed and starts to brown—an additional 2 to 3 minutes.

Add 10 cups cold water, Bovril, tomato paste, bay leaf, Worcestershire sauce, basil, black pepper, and peas. Bring to a boil. Reduce heat and simmer for 2 hours.

Add carrots, potatoes, cabbage, and parsley and continue to simmer for an additional 30 minutes.

Note: Peas will be softer if soaked overnight in quadruple their volume of cold water. If you prefer a more liquid to vegetable ratio, you can add a 10 ounce can of beef broth at the end of the cooking time.

	Each serving provides:		
241	Calories	30 g	Carbohydrate
23 g	Protein	398 mg	Sodium
4 g	Total fat	38 mg	Cholesterol

Beef, Bean, and Vegetable Soup

Sweet potatoes and yams are now prized as some of the healthiest vegetables you can eat. Unless they're baked until tender and slathered with lots of fresh butter, however, we would just as soon derive the benefits of these tuberous vegetables in the following soup.

Makes 8 to 10 servings

1¹/₂	cups white navy beans
1	pound lean ground beef
1	large onion, chopped
1	clove garlic, minced
1	can (28 ounces) diced tomatoes
3	cans (10 ounces each) beef broth plus 6 cups water (use water from beans plus additional water to make 6 cups)
4	stalks celery with leaves, chopped
2	carrots, thinly sliced or chopped
1	sweet potato or yam, diced (about 3 cups)
	pinch of cloves
	pinch of dry mustard
4	tablespoons minced fresh parsley
¹/₂	small cabbage, shredded
¹/₂	teaspoon black pepper

Rinse and soak beans overnight (or use the quick-soak method, page 20).

Spray bottom of Dutch oven with nonstick cooking spray and brown ground beef over medium heat, breaking up with a fork. Add onion and garlic and cook until onion is soft. Drain the beans and add to the beef mixture. Add tomatoes, beef broth, and water. Bring to a boil. Reduce heat and simmer for 1 hour.

Add the remaining vegetables and the spices, and simmer for an additional 30 to 35 minutes or until vegetables are tender. (We sometimes add a pinch of salt or a tablespoon of liquid Bovril, but taste it first—you may just love it as is!)

Note: This soup will thicken when it sits overnight. Add additional beef broth or stock if necessary. Never add water to finished soups— use stock (vegetable or beef). For this purpose, it is a good idea to save leftover vegetable water in the refrigerator. If it is not used in 2 to 3 days, store it in the freezer.

Each serving provides:

297	Calories	39 g	Carbohydrate
18 g	Protein	207 mg	Sodium
9 g	Total fat	31 mg	Cholesterol

Mexican Meatball Soup

This soup is full of flavor, full of protein, and full of fiber, and it is just the
remedy for a cold and otherwise uneventful evening. Team it up with some
hot cornbread, and your day will have a happy ending!

Makes 8 to 10 servings

Meatballs
1	pound extra-lean ground beef
3/4	cup fresh whole wheat bread crumbs (about 1 slice whole wheat bread)
3	tablespoons chopped fresh parsley
1/4	cup 2 percent evaporated canned milk
1	teaspoon cumin
1/2	teaspoon chili powder
1/2	teaspoon no-salt seasoning (page 260) or salt
1/8	teaspoon cayenne pepper

Soup
1	tablespoon olive oil
3	medium onions, finely chopped (about 3 1/2 cups)
1	medium to large green pepper, seeded and chopped
3	large cloves garlic, minced
2	tablespoons whole wheat flour
2	tablespoons liquid Bovril or instant beef stock
1 1/2	cups dry red wine
1	can (28 ounces) diced tomatoes
1	teaspoon dried oregano
1/2	teaspoon sugar

To make the meatballs, preheat the oven to 400°. Place all of the
meatball ingredients into a bowl and mix well. Form into 1-inch balls
(this makes about 42 meatballs). Lightly spray a cookie sheet with
nonstick cooking spray, place meatballs on the sheet, and bake for
10 minutes. Set aside until ready to add to soup.

Spoon olive oil into a Dutch oven or heavy-bottomed soup pot.
Add onion, green pepper, and garlic. Turn on heat to high; when vegetables start cooking, stir well, cover, then turn heat to low and cook
for 10 minutes (this procedure is called "sweating").

Remove cover, sprinkle whole wheat flour over top, then stir well. Gradually stir in 4 cups hot water, Bovril, and wine. Add the tomatoes, oregano, and sugar, cover, and simmer for 1 hour.

Add cooked meatballs, cover, and simmer for an additional 30 minutes.

Each serving provides:

180	Calories	13 g	Carbohydrate
10 g	Protein	464 mg	Sodium
9 g	Total fat	28 mg	Cholesterol

Judy and Bill's Leftover Salad Soup

*This is hardly a recipe and has nothing to do with beef, but we felt you should
know about it, so it had to be included in the book. Good friends in southern
California introduced us to this neat way of utilizing leftover salad that
hasn't been covered with fattening salad dressing, and it is simply delicious.
It varies, just as salads vary. Judy and Bill serve it cold, but try it hot on
chilly days. It is good both ways.*

*Can you believe something so simple and practical has escaped you all of
these years?*

Makes 1 serving

    leftover salad (yes, that wilted mass of vitamins and minerals
    you were going the feed to your garbage disposal)
1   cup tomato juice or V-8 juice

Simply put leftover salad into a blender with tomato juice. Blend
until smooth. Serve chilled or heated.

Each serving provides:			
74	Calories	17 g	Carbohydrate
4 g	Protein	897 mg	Sodium
0 g	Total fat	0 mg	Cholesterol

Minestrone

A loaf of crusty bread, a jug of wine, and thou—plus a huge bowl of this soup. Not a bad way to spend an evening!

Makes 8 servings

1	pound extra-lean ground beef
2	medium onions, finely chopped
2	medium carrots, diced
1	can (28 ounces) tomatoes
3	beef bouillon cubes
1/2	teaspoon black pepper
1 1/2	teaspoons thyme
1	teaspoon no-salt seasoning (page 260) or salt
1	medium zucchini, thinly sliced (roughly 2 cups)
2	cups chopped broccoli
1	can (19 ounces) garbanzo beans (chickpeas), drained
1	cup small shell macaroni or spaghetti broken into fourths

Brown beef in a large Dutch oven or soup pot over moderately high heat. Stir in onion and continue to cook for an additional 5 minutes.

Add carrots, tomatoes, 8 cups of water, bouillon cubes, pepper, thyme, and salt seasoning. Simmer, covered, for 1 hour.

Add zucchini, broccoli, garbanzo beans, and pasta. Simmer for an additional 10 to 15 minutes.

Note: Freshly grated Parmesan cheese sprinkled on top of the soup is delicious but adds to the fat content. We sometimes add some finely chopped sun-dried tomatoes (roughly 1/3 cup). They are fat-free and full of flavor.

	Each serving provides:		
316	Calories	37 g	Carbohydrate
19 g	Protein	663 mg	Sodium
11 g	Total fat	39 mg	Cholesterol

Diet Soup (Winter)

"Mirror, mirror on the wall, who is the thinnest one of all? Not me you say?"
Oh dear, well maybe this soup will help. This is a terrific way to kick-start
your diet. Have a bowl whenever you're hungry. It's filling without being
fattening (60 calories is nothing—about the same as two soda crackers).
If you have a bowl before dinner, you will eat far less and still be satisfied.

Makes 6 to 8 servings

1	cup finely chopped onion
4	cloves garlic, finely chopped
1	large tomato, chopped
1	small green pepper, seeded and chopped
1/2	teaspoon pepper
1	teaspoon caraway seeds
2	cans (10 ounces each) beef broth, undiluted
1	can (10 ounces) onion soup, undiluted
1	tablespoon white wine vinegar
1	packet artificial sweetener (such as Sugar Twin)
1	small head cabbage, coarsely shredded
4	cups cold water
1	teaspoon Bovril or instant beef stock

Place all ingredients in a large soup pot. Add 4 cups of water. Bring
to a boil. Reduce heat and simmer for about 25 to 30 minutes.

Note: If this soup is helping you lose weight, but you are getting a
bit tired of it, add 1 or 2 cans of green beans or wax beans, processed
in the food processor. It will change the texture and flavor slightly
without adding too many more calories.

Each serving provides:

60	Calories	12 g	Carbohydrate
4 g	Protein	651 mg	Sodium
1 g	Total fat	0 mg	Cholesterol

Diet Soup (Summer)

The weather is hot, you have just had a good look at yourself in your bathing suit, and that's it! This cold gazpacho-type soup is low in both fat and calories. Eat as much as you want. The pounds will disappear!

Makes 8 to 10 servings

2	cans (14 ounces each) crushed tomatoes
1	teaspoon low-salt beef granules
1	can (48 ounces) V8 juice
1	green pepper, seeded and diced
1	onion, diced
1	English cucumber, diced
2	cloves garlic, minced
1	tablespoon chopped parsley
2	to 3 drops Tabasco
1	tablespoon extra-virgin olive oil
2	tablespoons red wine vinegar
3/4	cup lowfat croutons, optional (see page 252)

Place crushed tomatoes and their juice in a large bowl. Dissolve beef granules in 2 tablespoons hot water and add to the bowl.

Add all remaining ingredients except croutons. Refrigerate for at least 4 hours or overnight.

Serve in chilled bowls and top with a sprinkle of croutons.

Each serving provides:

74	Calories	14 g	Carbohydrate
2 g	Protein	670 mg	Sodium
2 g	Total fat	0 mg	Cholesterol

Barbecuing or Broiling

Barbecuing became the most popular social custom of the summer, with people rushing out to buy whichever type barbecue would best suit their space and pocketbook. Some of today's models are so sophisticated, they don't even use charcoal. We can no longer rely on that great mixture of charcoal and smoke flavor that we anticipated each time the barbecue pit was fired up, because now we are told it may not be healthy. Drat! (The smoke was a result of the well-marbled steak fat melting and dripping down onto the coals, causing flare-ups.)

Marinades to the rescue! Marinades have been used for years to improve the quality of less-tender cuts (leaner cuts are usually the tougher cuts), and the good news is that we have many flavorful and tenderizing marinades to choose from. Select from among the many recipes in this section to satisfy discriminating appetites, both big and small. And may all your mosquitoes be little ones!

Here are some helpful hints:

- When marinating, you must prepare early in the day or the day before. Marinating helps to tenderize some cuts of meat.
- In most marinades, you can remove 3/4 of the oil and replace it with broth, wine, or fruit juice (not in our marinades, though—we have already done it for you). Always place marinades in glass or other nonmetal containers (wine will turn sour in a metal bowl). Sealable plastic bags can be used successfully.
- When barbecuing steak, a quick temperature test can be performed by placing your palm about 4 inches away from the fire. If it's too hot to hold your hand there for more than 2 seconds, your fire is ready. A holding time of 3 to 5 seconds will give you a medium to low heat.
- Use tongs for turning steaks rather than a fork, to prevent piercing the meat and letting valuable juices escape.
- A water pistol makes a great barbecue accessory, for extinguishing any flare-ups.
- You don't have to be an Escoffier to throw a steak on the grill—the trick is in knowing when to take it off! Barbecuing involves hair-trigger timing. Cooking times vary with thickness of steaks and desired doneness. The simplest test for doneness is the "fingertip" test. If the steak is soft to the touch, it is rare. If it springs back, it is medium. If it is firm, it is well done (and ruined, as far as these two carnivores are concerned!).

Here is a guideline with approximate times for *each side* on a preheated barbecue over medium heat (but keep the variables in mind, for example, cooking on a hot summer night versus a chilly fall or winter night, or whether the meat is at room temperature or straight from the refrigerator).

- A 1/2-inch to 3/4-inch steak will take 3 minutes for rare, 5 minutes for medium, and 7 minutes for well done.
- A 1-inch steak will take 5 minutes for rare, 6 minutes for medium, and 8 minutes for well done.
- A 1 1/2-inch steak will take 8 minutes for rare, 10 minutes for medium, and 12 minutes for well done.
- A 2-inch steak will take 15 minutes for rare, 18 minutes for medium, and 20 minutes for well done.

Broiling

The secret to successful broiling is to use a broiler pan specifically designed to match the distance from the broiler with the shelf arrangement of the oven. Meat should be positioned approximately 4 to 5 inches below the broiler. Broiler pans reduce smoking by allowing fat to drip into the bottom of the pan, away from the heat source. Once you trim fat from beef, the chance of flare-ups is greatly reduced.

Always preheat an electric broiler until the element is red hot. Remove the broiler pan *before* preheating, as meat will stick to a hot pan.

Broiling must be done with the door open to prevent the meat from baking. For a 3/4-inch to 1-inch steak, broil 5 to 6 minutes per side for rare and 7 to 8 minutes per side for medium (these timings are based on steaks positioned 4 to 5 inches below the broiler).

The less tender cuts of beef must be marinated to ensure tenderness. Pouch packs are now available that work very well, but making your own marinade is not difficult and is more economical. Something acidic is needed to soften connective tissues; wine, soy sauce, citrus juices, cider vinegar, and beer all work well. Oil is used as an adherent, so blot meat on paper towels before cooking to remove any excess oil. Remember to pierce meat with a long-tined fork, thus allowing the marinade to penetrate.

Shish Kebobs

Use separate skewers for meat and vegetables. Cherry tomatoes and mushrooms are favorites for shish kebobs, but unless your preferred doneness for meat is rare or medium rare, stick with green pepper and onions if you plan to cook vegetables on the same skewer. If you plan to use whole mushrooms on kebobs, pour boiling water over them and let them sit in the water until they can be skewered without splitting (up to 5 minutes, depending on the size of mushroom). Tiny new potatoes can be used on shish kebobs, but they must be parboiled first.

Tender cuts such as sirloin, tenderloin, and rib eye require as little as 20 minutes to marinate. The less tender cuts such as round steak, sirloin tip, and blade require much longer: 4 to 8 hours, or overnight.

If you're using wooden skewers, soak them in hot water first to prevent burning. If you're using metal skewers, spray them with non-stick cooking spray before assembly.

Thread meat loosely, leaving a small space between cubes for even cooking. Leave a space at the end for ease in turning.

Lightly spray the grill with nonstick cooking oil to help prevent sticking.

Steak Seasoning

When steak has been rubbed with a seasoning mixture, the rub creates a flavorful, slightly crunchy crust on the outside, while the inside retains its own distinct flavor.

Makes enough seasoning for 1 good-size steak

1   clove garlic, peeled and cut in half
1   teaspoon olive oil
1   teaspoon dry mustard
1   teaspoon sugar
     freshly ground black pepper

Rub each steak with a cut piece of garlic. Spread a thin film of olive oil on the steak. Combine mustard and sugar and sprinkle both sides of steak with this mixture.

Just before placing on well preheated barbecue, sprinkle steak with black pepper. Grill peppered side, pepper uncooked side, turn steak, then grill to desired doneness.

Each serving provides:

63	Calories	4 g	Carbohydrate
1 g	Protein	0 mg	Sodium
5 g	Total fat	0 mg	Cholesterol

Simple Hamburgers

What can we say about a hamburger? It's hardly gourmet, but every once in a while you just have to have one. Most people prefer to make them at home. Hamburgers are available in every city in North America in various shapes, sizes, and prices, ranging from a couple of dollars at McDonald's to $21.50 at the "21" Club in New York.

The dried minced onions give the flavor of fried onions without the fat.

Makes 4 patties

1   pound lean ground beef
1/4   teaspoon black pepper
1/2   teaspoon salt or no-salt seasoning (see page 260)
1   teaspoon dried minced onions

Mix ground beef, pepper, salt, and dried onions. Divide the mixture into 4 equal portions and shape into patties.

Place on barbecue for about 4 to 6 minutes on each side over moderately hot heat, or until cooked to your liking.

Each serving provides:

249	Calories	0 g	Carbohydrate
25 g	Protein	333 mg	Sodium
16 g	Total fat	81 mg	Cholesterol

Constanzia's Compromise Burgers

Connie, born in Italy, married a man from Hawaii. She loved hamburgers; he hated them. This was her compromise.

Makes 2 servings

Hamburgers
1/2	pound ground round steak, rump, sirloin, or any very lean beef
3	tablespoons chopped onion
1	egg
3	tablespoons bread crumbs
2	pineapple slices
2	large slices of Italian bread, toasted

Sauce
1	cup tomato sauce
1	tablespoon ketchup
1	tablespoon brown sugar
1	tablespoon lemon juice
	pinch of dry mustard
	pinch of ground cloves
	dash or two of Worcestershire sauce

Mix ground beef, onion, egg, and bread crumbs. Form into 2 patties and set aside.

Combine all of the sauce ingredients in a small saucepan. Simmer for 2 to 3 minutes.

Barbecue or broil the patties to medium rare. Also broil or barbecue the pineapple slices. Toast the bread slices. Dredge the cooked beef patties in the sauce, then place each one on a slice of Italian bread and top with pineapple. Spoon additional sauce over top.

Each serving provides:

502	Calories	47 g	Carbohydrate
33 g	Protein	1156 mg	Sodium
20 g	Total fat	187 mg	Cholesterol

David's Ginger Steak

When David serves this steak, he swears that it originated with the famous spy Mata Hari and that she elicited more secrets from her clientele over this dish than she ever did in her boudoir!

This is excellent served cold the following day.

Makes 4 to 6 servings

1/2	cup dark soy sauce
3/4	cup robust red wine
4	tablespoons grated fresh ginger
3	tablespoons grated fresh garlic
2 1/2	inch to 3-inch-thick piece of sirloin (this is roughly 2 to 2 1/2 pounds)

Combine soy sauce, wine, ginger, and garlic in a nonmetallic container. Place meat in this marinade and let sit for 4 to 8 hours, turning several times.

Broil or barbecue the meat for 7 to 9 minutes per side for medium rare (see note). It will blacken and char on the outside, which only contributes to the great flavor. Baste with the marinade frequently while cooking. Let the steak sit for 5 minutes before slicing, to allow juices to settle. Spoon some of the heated marinade on very thin slices of this sapid treat.

Note: When cooking the meat, 7 to 9 minutes per side should suffice for medium rare, but you should test with a sharp knife in the center to confirm. Broiling may take a little longer than barbecuing, as you must remove the meat from the heat when basting frequently.

Each serving provides:			
244	Calories	2 g	Carbohydrate
37 g	Protein	774 mg	Sodium
8 g	Total fat	104 mg	Cholesterol

Shish Kebobs

We have seen this dish spelled Kabobs and Kebabs—they all mean roasting meat on a stick. The word originates from two Turkish words: sis, meaning sword, and kebab, meaning roasted meat. (See our tips on cooking shish kebobs at the beginning of this chapter.)

This is delicious served with risotto and marinated vegetables in tomato baskets (page 258) or broiled zucchini (page 248).

Makes 4 to 6 servings

3/4	cup red wine (a Burgundy is nice)
2	tablespoons olive oil
1/2	teaspoon salt
1	small onion, finely chopped
1/2	teaspoon dried thyme
2	to 3 tablespoons peppercorns
11/2	pounds boneless sirloin, cut into 1-inch cubes

Combine wine, oil, salt, onion, thyme, and peppercorns in a glass bowl or sealable bag just large enough to hold meat. Add beef, cover or seal, and refrigerate for 2 to 3 hours (see note).

Thread beef onto skewers (if wooden, make sure you soak in water for several hours to prevent excessive charring). Grill on a preheated barbecue over medium heat for 10 to 15 minutes or until desired doneness. Turn often to brown evenly.

Note: If you use a less tender cut, such as inside or outside round, sirloin tip, or blade, increase marinating time to a minimum of 4 hours or, preferably, overnight.

If you would like a "peppery" snap to your kebobs, keep the peppercorns separate, then crack them with the flat side of a knife blade and spread on a flat surface. Thread marinated steak cubes on skewers and roll lightly in pepper just before barbecuing.

Each serving provides:

219	Calories	1 g	Carbohydrate
30 g	Protein	108 mg	Sodium
10 g	Total fat	87 mg	Cholesterol

Broiled Bombay Beef

We have a friend, an amateur chef, who confessed that his set of skewers had been for years in the back of his utility drawer, unused, until he started to prepare this dish. He now keeps them in the front of the drawer.

Serve this with rice, baby carrots, and a fresh green salad.

Makes 4 to 6 servings

1/4	cup soy sauce
2	tablespoons honey
3	cloves garlic, minced
2	teaspoons curry powder
1	teaspoon sesame seeds
1/2	teaspoon cumin
2	tablespoons olive oil
2	pounds rump steak, cut into 1-inch cubes

Combine the soy sauce, honey, garlic, curry powder, sesame seeds, cumin, and oil in a bowl. Marinate the meat for a minimum of 4 hours, but all day or overnight is best. Stir occasionally.

When ready to cook, skewer the meat and broil for about 10 minutes, turning 2 or 3 times during the cooking process. Meat should be medium-rare.

Note: If you prefer more rare than medium, push pieces closer together; for more well done, space meat pieces a little further apart. Be careful if you use wooden skewers, even if you have soaked them in water before, which is a must.

Each serving provides:

263	Calories	2 g	Carbohydrate
38 g	Protein	257 mg	Sodium
11 g	Total fat	100 mg	Cholesterol

Ground Beef Kebobs, Chinese-Style

When cooking these kebobs, spray the grill with nonstick cooking spray before heating and again just before you cook the kebobs. Use a spatula to turn the meatballs, to avoid breaking them. When they're done, they will be picture perfect!

Makes 3 to 4 servings

Kebobs

1	pound lean ground beef
2	tablespoons Worcestershire sauce
2	tablespoons yellow mustard (hot dog mustard!)
1	tablespoon lite soy sauce
1	large green or red pepper, seeded and cut into chunks
1	can (14 ounces) pineapple chunks, drained (reserve juice)

Sweet and Sour Sauce

1	tablespoon cornstarch
3	tablespoons white vinegar
2	tablespoons prepared mustard
$1/2$	cup pineapple juice (reserved from canned pineapple)
$1/2$	cup brown sugar, firmly packed
1	teaspoon Worcestershire sauce

Combine ground beef, Worcestershire sauce, mustard, and soy sauce in a bowl. Mix thoroughly and shape into 12 balls.

Assemble the kebobs: alternate 3 meatballs, green pepper chunks, and pineapple chunks on each of 4 skewers. (If you use metal skewers, spray the skewers with nonstick cooking spray before assembling kebobs.) Set aside.

To make the sauce, dissolve cornstarch in vinegar, then combine it with the mustard, pineapple juice, brown sugar, and Worcestershire sauce in a small saucepan. Stir well to dissolve sugar. Simmer until sauce thickens. Keep warm.

Grill kebobs until cooked to desired doneness, turning several times.

Serve the kebobs and sauce over hot, fluffy rice.

Each serving provides:

457	Calories	51 g	Carbohydrate
26 g	Protein	506 mg	Sodium
17 g	Total fat	81 mg	Cholesterol

Bob's Marinated Chuck Roast

Makes 8 to 10 servings

1	medium onion, finely chopped
2	tablespoons canola oil or safflower oil
2	large cloves garlic, minced
1/3	cup lite soy sauce
1	teaspoon ground allspice
1	teaspoon powdered ginger
1	teaspoon rosemary
3	tablespoons red wine vinegar
2	tablespoons brown sugar
1	can (10 ounces) low-sodium beef broth, undiluted
2	to 4 pounds chuck roast, cut a minimum of 1^1/$_2$ inches thick (have the butcher cut it for you)

In a small saucepan sauté onion in oil until soft. Stir in garlic, soy sauce, allspice, ginger, rosemary, vinegar, brown sugar, and beef broth and bring to a boil. Remove from heat and cool. (The marinade may be made a day or two ahead and refrigerated.)

Place meat in a deep glass bowl or sealable heavy plastic bag and add marinade. Marinate meat overnight, turning occasionally.

Remove meat from marinade and bring to room temperature before cooking. Barbecue or broil at high heat for about 8 minutes per side, or at medium heat for about 10 to 12 minutes per side, turning once (a steak thicker than 1^1/$_2$ inches will take slightly longer).

Slice roast at an angle into ^{1}/$_4$-inch slices and serve.

Each serving provides:

207	Calories	2 g	Carbohydrate
24 g	Protein	135 mg	Sodium
11 g	Total fat	82 mg	Cholesterol

Herbed London Broil

Flank steak must be served medium rare (or rare), as it tends to be a little on the tough side if overdone.

Serve with herbed new potatoes, fresh green beans, and a sliced tomato salad.

Makes 8 servings

2	pounds flank steak
$1/2$	teaspoon salt
$1/2$	teaspoon pepper
$1/4$	teaspoon basil
$1/4$	teaspoon rosemary
$1/2$	teaspoon garlic powder
$1/2$	onion, very finely chopped
2	tablespoons red wine vinegar
3	tablespoons vegetable oil

To score meat on both sides: make diagonal slashes with a sharp knife about one-fourth of the way into the flesh, then do the same in the opposite direction so you have created "diamonds" about 1 inch wide; turn steak and do the same on the opposite side.

Place steak in a flat dish. Combine the salt, pepper, basil, rosemary, garlic powder, onion, vinegar, and oil and pour over steak, turning meat several times to coat well. Let sit for roughly 3 hours.

Preheat broiler. Broil meat 3 to 4 inches from the heat for 5 minutes on one side and 3 to 4 minutes on the other.

To serve, cut in thin slices diagonally across the grain.

Each serving provides:

270	Calories	2 g	Carbohydrate
26 g	Protein	211 mg	Sodium
18 g	Total fat	66 mg	Cholesterol

Barbecued or Broiled Marinated Flank Steak #1

Makes 8 servings

2	pounds flank steak
1	small onion, peeled and sliced
1	teaspoon grated lemon peel
1/2	cup freshly squeezed lemon juice (you can use bottled juice in a pinch)
2	tablespoons sugar
1/2	teaspoon salt
1 1/2	teaspoons crushed oregano
1 1/2	teaspoons coarsely ground black pepper
2	tablespoons lite soy sauce

Remove all visible fat and as much membrane from the steak as possible. Score meat on both sides (for a description of scoring, see the previous recipe for Herbed London Broil). Place the meat in a plastic bag with the onion.

Combine the grated lemon peel, lemon juice, sugar, salt, oregano, pepper, and soy sauce and pour over the meat. Let marinate for at least 3 hours before barbecuing.

Cook to medium or medium rare. To serve, slice diagonally against the grain.

Each serving provides:

225	Calories	2 g	Carbohydrate
26 g	Protein	148 mg	Sodium
12 g	Total fat	66 mg	Cholesterol

Barbecued or Broiled Marinated Flank Steak #2

This marinade has a bit of oil, but it's a real family favorite.

Makes 6 to 8 servings

1^1/$_2$	to 2 pounds flank steak
3	tablespoons canola oil or safflower oil
4	tablespoons lite soy sauce
2	teaspoons brown sugar
^{1}/$_4$	teaspoon ground ginger
^{1}/$_4$	teaspoon black pepper
1	clove garlic, minced (or ^{1}/$_4$ teaspoon garlic powder)

Remove all visible fat and as much membrane from the steak as possible. Score meat on both sides (for a description of scoring, see the earlier recipe for Herbed London Broil). Place in a shallow dish just large enough to accommodate the meat.

Combine the oil, soy sauce, brown sugar, ginger, pepper, and garlic and pour over the meat. Let marinate for 3 hours, turning occasionally.

Remove steak from marinade and broil for 5 minutes on one side and 3 to 4 minutes on the other. It should be medium rare (flank steak should not be too rare or too well done).

Each serving provides:

232	Calories		1 g	Carbohydrate
26 g	Protein		157 mg	Sodium
13 g	Total fat		66 mg	Cholesterol

Overnight Marinated Flank Steak

We felt that three recipes for flank steak were probably enough but we couldn't agree on which one to leave out, so now we have four. (Actually, we have five if you include the beer marinade variation below.) Serve the flank steak pleasantly pink with a medley of al dente vegetables.

Beer-marinated flank steak (see variation below) is great served on French bread with sautéed onions and no-fat sour cream mixed with horseradish. To sauté onions, spray a nonstick skillet with nonstick cooking spray and sprinkle on a bit of paprika, which helps in the browning process.

Makes 6 to 8 servings

1 1/2	to 2 pounds flank steak
3/4	cup maple syrup
2	tablespoons soy sauce
1/4	cup vinegar
1/2	teaspoon black pepper
1	clove garlic, minced

Trim meat of any visible fat and score as in the previous recipes. Combine maple syrup, soy sauce, vinegar, pepper, and garlic and pour over the meat. Marinate the meat overnight, turning occasionally.

When you're ready to cook, drain and save the marinade. Broil steak 5 minutes on first side and 4 minutes on opposite side.

Meanwhile, heat remaining marinade and serve with the meat. Remember to always slice flank steak diagonally across the grain.

Variation

Beer Marinade: If you want the simplest of marinades—just use beer. Marinate the flank steak for 24 hours; then barbecue to medium rare.

Each serving provides:			
295	Calories	20 g	Carbohydrate
26 g	Protein	339 mg	Sodium
12 g	Total fat	66 mg	Cholesterol

Leslie's Hawaiian Tidbits

Leslie and her husband, Scot, were the first to bring the "Maui Ribs" recipe back to North America from Hawaii. Lifestyles have changed since then, so these tidbits have replaced the fat-laden (but so good) ribs.

The tidbits can be served as an appetizer or main course.

Makes 4 servings

1	pound flank steak
1/2	cup pineapple juice (reserved from the tidbits below)
1/4	cup brown sugar
1/4	teaspoon white pepper
1/2	teaspoon ground ginger
1/4	teaspoon garlic salt
1/2	teaspoon no-salt seasoning (see page 260)
1/4	cup soy sauce
1	tablespoon red wine vinegar
1/2	cup pineapple tidbits

Trim flank steak of all visible fat and cut across the grain into 1/3-inch strips.

Combine the pineapple juice, brown sugar, pepper, ginger, garlic salt, no-salt seasoning, soy sauce, and vinegar and pour over the flank steak. Sprinkle with tidbits. Cover and marinate overnight or up to 4 days in the refrigerator.

Barbecue on a hot grill for 1 to 2 minutes per side. Strips may also be strung on skewers and cooked for roughly 3 to 4 minutes per side. (If you use bamboo skewers, be sure to soak them in hot water for 10 minutes before assembling.)

Each serving provides:			
286	Calories	17 g	Carbohydrate
26 g	Protein	658 mg	Sodium
12 g	Total fat	66 mg	Cholesterol

Jamaican Jerk Burgers

Jerk seasoning is a fairly new spice in North America and seems to be catching on in popularity. If your supermarket does not carry it, you can make your own, which is a lot more economical, providing you have the spices on hand. One of our young friends, who was three days overdue with her first child, ate two of these and promptly gave birth that very night. Coincidence? Maybe!

Makes 4 servings

1   pound lean ground beef

Jerk Seasoning
2   tablespoons paprika
3   teaspoons oregano
2   teaspoons dried chili peppers
1   teaspoon garlic powder
1   teaspoon garlic salt
1   teaspoon black pepper
1/2   teaspoon cayenne pepper
1/2   teaspoon dry mustard
1   teaspoon nutmeg

Combine paprika, oregano, dried peppers, garlic powder, garlic salt, black pepper, cayenne pepper, mustard, and nutmeg. If you're making the jerk seasoning ahead of time, store in a small jar.

Divide meat into 4 portions and shape into hamburger patties.

Put 2 teaspoons of the jerk seasoning on a large piece of waxed paper or foil and spread out. Place patties on top, pressing down slightly. Turn patties over and sprinkle any remaining seasoning over top, pressing gently into the meat.

Barbecue the patties for roughly 4 minutes on each side over moderately high heat.

Make sure you spray the grill well with nonstick cooking spray before the grill heats up and just again before placing patties on to cook. Use a spatula or tongs when turning patties to prevent piercing and loss of natural juices.

Each serving provides:

247	Calories	0 g	Carbohydrate
25 g	Protein	207 mg	Sodium
16 g	Total fat	81 mg	Cholesterol

Fajitas

Invite your favorite conquistador for this backyard fun food. Also check out Kathy's Fiery Fajitas (using ground beef) on page 170.

Makes 6 servings

Fajitas

1¹/₂	pounds flank steak
2	tablespoons olive oil
	juice of 2 limes (about 6 tablespoons)
¹/₄	cup red wine vinegar
¹/₄	cup chopped fresh cilantro or chopped onions
1	teaspoon sugar
¹/₂	teaspoon oregano
2	cloves garlic, minced
1	teaspoon cumin
¹/₄	teaspoon salt
6	flour tortillas

Toppings

1	large tomato, diced
1	medium red onion, cut into slivers and stir-fried (see note)
1	small sweet green pepper, cut into strips and stir-fried (see note)
1	small red pepper, cut into strips and stir-fried (see note)
¹/₄	to ¹/₂ head of lettuce, shredded
¹/₂	cup non-fat sour cream
1	cup shredded lowfat cheddar cheese
1	cup salsa, mild or hot

Remove all visible fat from steak and score on both sides.

Combine oil, lime juice, vinegar, cilantro, sugar, oregano, garlic, cumin, and salt in a shallow baking dish just large enough to hold the meat. Marinate the meat for 4 hours, turning occasionally.

Remove the meat from the marinade and barbecue so the meat is cooked to medium. Or, broil for 5 minutes, turn, and broil for 4 minutes (meat should be medium).

Warm tortillas by following the package directions, or wrap in a damp tea towel and place in a 350° oven for 15 to 20 minutes. (Lightly steamed pita bread can be substituted for the tortillas.)

Slice the steak diagonally across the grain into thin slices. Place on a large platter and serve with warmed flour tortillas and any or all of the toppings. To compile the fajitas, spoon the beef down the center of a warmed tortilla and add desired toppings. Fold bottom of tortilla up and then fold sides in to enclose filling. Eat from your hand.

Note: When stir-frying, use nonstick cooking spray. If vegetables begin to stick while cooking, add 1 or 2 drops of water. Don't overcook.

	Each serving provides:		
433	Calories	30 g	Carbohydrate
36 g	Protein	516 mg	Sodium
19 g	Total fat	80 mg	Cholesterol

Chinese Steak Salad

Putting a salad recipe in the barbecue section might be awkward, but we agreed that this is where it belongs. You will enjoy the unique textures and flavors of this one-dish meal. This recipe is courtesy of Canada's Beef Information Centre.

Makes 4 to 6 servings

	seasoning packet from instant noodles (below)
1/4	cup pineapple juice
3	tablespoons steak sauce
1/4	cup soy sauce
1/4	cup sesame oil
2	tablespoons white vinegar
2	teaspoons sugar
1 1/2	teaspoons grated fresh ginger
1	pound "inside round" steak
1	small head Chinese cabbage (napa or suey choy), thinly sliced
1	red pepper, seeded and chopped
1	package (3 ounces) Oriental instant noodles (beef flavor), broken up (see note)
1	package (4 ounces) slivered almonds, toasted
1/4	cup sesame seeds, toasted

Prepare marinade by combining powdered seasonings packet that came in the instant noodles with pineapple juice, steak sauce, soy sauce, sesame oil, vinegar, sugar, and ginger.

Trim steak of any visible external fat and place in a nonmetal dish. Pour marinade over steak, cover, and marinate in the refrigerator for 3 to 4 hours or overnight.

Drain steak and reserve marinade to make the salad dressing.

Grill or broil steak until medium rare, approximately 5 minutes per side.

Meanwhile, bring marinade/dressing to a boil in a saucepan and simmer for 5 minutes. Toss cabbage, pepper, noodles, almonds, and sesame seeds with hot dressing.

Slice steak thinly and fan strips on top of the salad. Serve with crusty rolls.

Note: Noodles should be crunchy, not cooked.

Each serving provides:				
443	Calories	23 g	Carbohydrate
27 g	Protein	1287 mg	Sodium
28 g	Total fat	56 mg	Cholesterol

Stove-Top

It is important to use heavy-duty, nonstick pots and pans with tight-fitting lids for lowfat cooking. Good pots and pans are a good investment! We have used a nonstick frying pan throughout this book; it is essential for top-of-the-stove cooking (we hesitate to use the word "frying," which has been deleted from the vocabularies of the rapidly increasing number of reformed fat-oholics).

By using herbs and spices, you can cut down considerably on the amount of salt required for a truly delicious dish. We have used some interesting and unusual ingredients to enhance the flavor in many of the dishes throughout this book. Who would expect to find cinnamon, coffee granules, or molasses in a beef cookbook? Your palate is in for a delightful surprise when you try these dishes

For perfectly cooked steaks (tenderloin, lean rib eye, or New York strip loin), heat a heavy, ungreased skillet and sear steaks quickly on both sides. Place meat, not touching, in a shallow baking pan and bake in a preheated 350° oven for 7 to 10 minutes. This timing is for 1-inch to 1½-inch steaks at room temperature. At 7 minutes, steaks will be rare; at 10 minutes, they will be medium rare. While the steaks are finishing in the oven, you have enough time to put the finishing touches on the vegetables, toss the salad, etc., so when the steaks are ready—so are you!

Roasts and Stews

Pot roasts and stew meats are cut from a much-exercised part of the animal and therefore are more fibrous and tough. Long simmering tenderizes the fibers. Beef should simmer, never boil; the difference is tender, compact meat versus dry and stringy.

Resting meat in a marinade helps to tenderize as well as add interesting and unusual flavors. Beer makes an excellent base for marinating beef, as does red wine. The temperature in cooking causes the alcohol to evaporate but you retain the subtle flavors that these beverages impart.

Chuck is the best cut for beef stew. Avoid meat that is already cut up and labeled "stew meat." You are better off buying a boneless chuck roast and cutting it up yourself (watch for the sales!). Make sure you cut off any connective tissue as well as fat. Your meat will be far more tender.

Here are some general tips for making stews.

Selecting the Beef

For extra-lean stew beef, buy outside round steak or hip beef. If you use blade, cross rib or shoulder, you must carefully trim the meat of any fat and sinew before cutting into cubes.

Browning

Browning the beef cubes before adding the liquid significantly improves both the color and flavor of the finished product. Once the meat is browned, some particles of meat and juices remain in the pan. Add liquid and heat until all these baked-on particles loosen. This process, called deglazing, provides a rich, robust base.

Coating the beef cubes with flour before cooking increases the amount of browning and helps to slightly thicken the liquid. Finely mincing the onion before sautéing adds a bit of substance to the liquid as well. Adding seasonings to the meat before browning enhances flavors.

For quicker preparation, the browning can be eliminated, particularly if the recipe uses a darkening ingredient such as tomato paste, soy sauce, or brown coloring agent. However, this method does not improve flavor.

Stock

The basic beef stew calls for beef stock. Making your own stock (see recipe on page 18) helps control the amount of salt used, but if this is not possible, look for low-sodium stocks. There are now low-salt instant beef granules or cubes available; dissolved in water, they are very convenient for today's busy cooks.

Tomato juice, tomato paste, or stewed tomatoes are a common addition to stews, giving the stock a rich color and a tangy taste. Red wine, sherry, and beer add very distinct flavors to stew.

Cooking

The amount of liquid varies, but there should always be enough liquid to just cover the meat. The less liquid, the more flavorful the broth. If you're going to add vegetables, you'll need more liquid. As a rule of thumb, plan on approximately 2 cups of liquid for every pound of beef.

Once the liquid has come to a boil, reduce the heat immediately so that the stew simmers, not boils. Simmer until beef is fork-tender, anywhere from 1½ to 2½ hours, depending on the size and cut of beef.

If you have used good lean beef, defatting should not be necessary. The best way to defat a stew is to let it cool; the fat will then rise to the surface and can be removed.

Vegetables and Dumplings

To maintain their color and shape, root vegetables such as potatoes, carrots, and turnips should be added in the last 30 to 40 minutes of cooking, but make sure they are cooked! Today's palates favor "crisp" vegetables, but you don't want crisp potatoes in your stew. Softer vegetables, such as peas and mushrooms (sautéed lightly in a nonstick skillet sprayed with nonstick cooking spray), should be added in the final minutes.

If you have never made dumplings, don't be intimidated. Follow our recipe for lowfat dumplings in our recipe for beef stew in this chapter (page 60). The secret to light dumplings is to steam them on top of simmering liquid and to never crowd the pan. Make sure the pot is sufficiently wide and deep so that the dumplings have a chance to expand. To test for doneness, insert a toothpick. If it comes out clean, the dumplings are done.

Beef Stew with Lowfat Dumplings

Browning the stew meat in the oven rather than frying on top of the stove eliminates the fat used for frying. Make sure you line the cookie sheet with foil for easy cleanup. Avoid over-crowding for even browning.

Makes 4 servings

Stew

1/4	cup whole wheat flour
1/2	plus 1/4 teaspoon paprika
1/2	teaspoon freshly ground black pepper
1 1/2	pounds lean stew meat
2	medium onions, chopped
2	cloves garlic, minced
1	tablespoon liquid Bovril or instant beef stock
3	carrots, cut in 1-inch pieces
2	celery ribs, cut in 1-inch pieces
1	large or 2 medium parsnips, cut in 1-inch pieces
2	tablespoons minced fresh parsley
1/2	teaspoon dried basil
1/4	teaspoon dried thyme
1/4	teaspoon cinnamon

Lowfat Dumplings

1	cup all-purpose flour
1	tablespoon baking powder
1/2	teaspoon salt
1 1/2	tablespoons canola oil or safflower oil

Preheat oven to 350°.

Combine flour, 1/2 teaspoon paprika, and pepper in a brown paper bag or plastic bag; shake beef pieces, a few at a time, in the seasoned flour. Place meat pieces on a foil-lined cookie sheet and bake for 20 minutes or until lightly browned. Save any remaining flour for later.

While beef is browning, spray bottom of a Dutch oven or stockpot well with a nonstick cooking spray and sauté onions, garlic, and 1/4 teaspoon paprika over medium heat until onions are soft, about 3 to 5 minutes. Be very careful this does not burn or your stew will be bitter. Stir frequently during this time.

Remove from heat and stir in any remaining seasoned flour. Empty browned beef cubes into pot and add 3 1/2 cups water. Add

Bovril, carrots, celery, parsnips, parsley, basil, thyme, and cinnamon. Cover and simmer gently until meat is tender, from 1 1/2 to 2 hours.

To make the dumplings, sift flour, baking powder, and salt into a medium-size bowl. Combine oil and 2/3 cup water and stir into dry ingredients only until blended.

Add dumpling mixture by spoonfuls over the simmering stew (you should have about 6 dumplings). Cook, tightly covered, for 15 minutes. Serve at once.

Note: The above dumpling recipe is foolproof, but if you want an even faster and easier recipe, mix 2 cups Bisquick with 2/3 cup milk; drop by spoonfuls on top of stew and cook uncovered over low heat for 10 minutes; cover, then cook for an additional 10 minutes (makes 8 dumplings). You can add an herb of your choice to flavor the dumplings, for example, parsley, thyme, or tarragon. (Thank you to Mary Kling for this tip.)

Each serving provides:

547	Calories	52 g	Carbohydrate
45 g	Protein	1008 mg	Sodium
17 g	Total fat	102 mg	Cholesterol

"Black" Beef Roast

This roast received raves when presented to our testers. Many guests went back for seconds (one guest really struggled, because the dessert was fresh peach pie, and he knew he did not have room for seconds plus the pie!).

Vinegar and coffee might sound like strange ingredients, but this combination produces the most wonderfully tender and flavorful meat. The dark delicious pan gravy has no trace of vinegar or coffee, and we guarantee you will make this roast again.

Mashed potatoes are a must with this dish. Green beans or peas and mashed turnips make this a perfect "meat and potatoes" meal.

Makes 6 servings

4	pounds top round or rump roast
1/2	medium-size onion, peeled and cut into slivers
2	cloves garlic, peeled and cut into slivers
1	cup apple cider vinegar
1	tablespoon olive oil
3	cups strong, brewed coffee

Trim any excess fat from meat, and using a long sharp knife, cut slits almost down to the bottom of the roast, but not all the way through. Insert slivers of onion and garlic into slits, pushing down well with your finger and filling up the slits. Place in a deep glass or stainless steel bowl. Pour vinegar over meat, making sure it runs down into the slits. Cover and place in the refrigerator for 24 to 48 hours.

Drain, discarding vinegar. Heat oil in a heavy-bottom Dutch oven or small heavy roasting pan with a tight-fitting lid over moderately high heat. Brown meat until nearly burned on all sides (this is important if you want great tasting gravy). Pour coffee and 1 cup water over top. Cover tightly and bring to a boil. As soon as liquid reaches a boil, immediately reduce heat to simmer and cook slowly for 4 to 4 1/2 hours, turning roast over halfway through cooking time. If heat is low enough (although it must be simmering) and lid is heavy enough, you should be left with lots of delicious dark gravy in the pan.

Note: If you like the gravy more sauce-like, remove the meat from the pot and keep warm. Dissolve 2 to 3 teaspoons cornstarch in 1/4 cup red wine or beef broth. Add to the liquid in the pot. Bring to a boil and boil for 2 to 3 minutes. Add a pinch of salt and pepper.

Each serving provides:

485	Calories	3 g	Carbohydrate
74 g	Protein	170 mg	Sodium
18 g	Total fat	209 mg	Cholesterol

Beer Stew with Chili Dumplings

Stews have been the mainstay of good home cooking for years. A good stew is the ultimate comfort food. This updated version ranks up there with the best of them.

   This recipe calls for garlic pepper, which is a useful seasoning to have on the shelf for lowfat cooking.

Makes 6 servings

Stew

1/4	cup all-purpose flour
1/2	teaspoon salt
1/2	teaspoon seasoned garlic pepper
1 1/2	pounds lean stewing beef, cut in 1-inch cubes
2	tablespoons vegetable oil
2	medium to large onions (about 1 1/2 pounds), minced
1/2	teaspoon thyme
1	bottle or can (12 ounces) beer
1	can (19 ounces) tomato juice
1	tablespoon brown sugar
2	tablespoons tomato paste (see note)
1	tablespoon Worcestershire sauce
1	bay leaf
4	carrots, cut in chunks
2	medium potatoes, peeled and quartered or cut in eighths
1	cup frozen peas

Chili Dumplings

1	cup flour
1	tablespoon baking powder
1/2	teaspoon garlic salt
1	teaspoon chili powder
1/8	teaspoon cayenne pepper
1 1/2	tablespoons vegetable oil
2/3	cup skim milk

Combine flour, salt, and garlic pepper in a bag. Shake beef cubes in the seasoned flour. Heat the oil in a Dutch oven and brown the meat over medium-high heat. Turn to brown all sides. Remove meat from pan and set aside. (If you have not used a pot with a nonstick base and meat is sticking, add 1 or 2 drops of beer, not more oil.)

Reduce heat and add the onions and thyme. Cook until soft and golden brown, about 3 to 5 minutes. Add beer, tomato juice, brown sugar, tomato paste, Worcestershire sauce, and bay leaf. Bring to a boil, reduce heat, and cover. Simmer for 1 hour, stirring once or twice.

Add carrots and potatoes and cook until tender, about 30 minutes.

Meanwhile, make the dumpling mixture: sift together the flour, baking powder, garlic salt, chili powder, and cayenne pepper. Combine the oil and the milk and add to the dry ingredients; mix only until the flour is absorbed.

Add the peas to the stew, and as soon as liquid returns to a boil, drop the dumpling mixture by large spoonfuls on top of the simmering stew (you should have about 6 dumplings). Cover tightly and simmer for an additional 15 minutes (do not lift lid). Remove bay leaf and serve at once.

Note: If you're going to open a can of tomato paste for 1 tablespoon, here's a good idea for the rest of the can. Lay a piece of plastic wrap on a cookie sheet and measure out the remaining can, 1 tablespoon at a time, onto a cookie sheet. Freeze, then wrap individually and store in a plastic bag in the freezer for future use.

Each serving provides:

536	Calories	60 g	Carbohydrate
34 g	Protein	1094 mg	Sodium
16 g	Total fat	68 mg	Cholesterol

Beef and Mushroom Stew
with Caraway Dumplings

This recipe is courtesy of Canada's Beef Information Centre.

Makes 4 to 6 servings

Stew

2	tablespoons all-purpose flour
1/2	teaspoon salt
1/2	teaspoon freshly ground black pepper
2	tablespoons vegetable oil
1 1/2	pounds lean stew beef, cut in 1-inch cubes
1/2	cup chopped onion
2	cloves garlic, minced
1	can (10 ounces) beef broth or consommé plus 1 can water, or 2 1/2 cups homemade beef stock
1/2	cup dry red wine
1	bay leaf
1/4	teaspoon thyme
1/2	pound small whole mushrooms
1	tablespoon butter

Caraway Dumplings

1	cup flour
2	teaspoons baking powder
1/2	teaspoon salt
1	teaspoon caraway seeds
1	egg
	about 1/2 cup milk

Combine flour, salt, and pepper in a bag. Shake beef cubes in seasoned flour to coat. Heat oil in a Dutch oven with a heavy bottom. Brown beef cubes over medium-high heat, turning to brown all sides.

Add onion and garlic and sauté over medium heat until soft, about 3 to 5 minutes. Stir in broth and water, wine, bay leaf, and thyme. Bring to a boil, stirring constantly. Cover, reduce heat, and simmer until meat is tender, about 1 1/2 to 2 hours.

Make the dumplings: combine flour, baking powder, salt, and caraway seeds in a small bowl. Beat egg in a 1-cup measuring cup. Add enough milk to egg to measure 1/2 cup. Pour egg-milk mixture into flour. Stir to form a stiff batter. Don't overmix. Drop mixture by spoonfuls onto top of simmering stew (you should have about 8 dumplings). Cover and steam for 10 minutes.

Just before serving, brown mushrooms in butter and add to stew.

Each serving provides:

379	Calories	24 g	Carbohydrate
32 g	Protein	839 mg	Sodium
16 g	Total fat	111 mg	Cholesterol

Minute Steaks, Sauerbraten-Style

Sauerbraten is a pot roast that needs to be marinated a few days ahead, so if you have a yen for the sweet-and-sour flavor of this popular German dish and no time to prepare it, you can pinch-hit with the following recipe. Serve with fresh frozen peas and mashed potatoes (instant will add to the speed of preparation of this wonderfully homey meal), and enjoy this meal on a chilly winter's night.

Makes 2 servings

1	tablespoon flour
1/2	teaspoon salt
1/2	teaspoon ground ginger
1/8	teaspoon black pepper
1/8	teaspoon ground cloves
1	tablespoon brown sugar
1	tablespoon instant onion flakes
2	tablespoons red wine vinegar
1/4	teaspoon Kitchen Bouquet (see note)
1	tablespoon butter
1	tablespoon olive oil
2	minute steaks (5 to 6 ounces each), all visible fat removed

Place flour, 1/2 cup water, salt, ginger, pepper, and cloves in a small jar and shake well.

Empty seasonings into small saucepan and stir in brown sugar, onion flakes, red wine vinegar, and Kitchen Bouquet. Cook over medium heat, stirring constantly, until mixture thickens. Set aside.

Heat butter and oil in a skillet large enough to hold both minute steaks. Cook steaks over high heat until browned on both sides (this will take only 1 to 2 minutes on each side). Remove meat to platter to keep warm.

Empty any fat residue in bottom of the pan, but not the brown bits that will cling after meat has cooked. Add 1/2 cup water to the pan and cook over high heat, stirring to loosen brown bits on bottom. Boil over high heat to reduce liquid to about half its original volume. Add sauce in saucepan to the skillet and stir until well heated. Pour over steaks and serve.

Note: Kitchen Bouquet is a browning sauce for meat and gravy. Liquid Bovril can be substituted, but its flavor is not as concentrated as Kitchen Bouquet.

Each serving provides:

375	Calories	14 g	Carbohydrate
36 g	Protein	687 mg	Sodium
19 g	Total fat	107 mg	Cholesterol

Boeuf Bourguignon

This dish is traditionally made with Burgundy wine. Serve with mashed potatoes or flat noodles and fresh asparagus.

Makes 4 servings

2	pounds bottom round steak, trimmed of all visible fat and sinew and cut into large cubes
1/2	teaspoon black pepper
1/2	teaspoon paprika
1	can (14 ounces) small onions, drained and well rinsed (see note)
1	tablespoon capers
1	teaspoon Dijon mustard or horseradish mustard
1	medium carrot, coarsely chopped
1	cup plus 2 tablespoons red wine
1/2	pound fresh mushroom caps
2	tablespoons brandy
2	tablespoons red wine
1	tablespoon cornstarch
	Salt, to taste

Sprinkle beef with black pepper and paprika. Spray a heavy-bottom Dutch oven with nonstick cooking spray. Add the beef and brown quickly over medium-high heat. Push meat to one side of the pan and pour in 1/4 cup water, stirring well to loosen brown bits.

Add onions, capers, Dijon mustard, carrot, and red wine. Cover and simmer gently for 2 hours, or until meat is tender. Add the mushroom caps and brandy and simmer gently for an additional 15 minutes.

Mix 2 tablespoons red wine with cornstarch and add to the stew. Cook, stirring gently, until sauce is thickened—this will take only a

minute or two. Adjust seasoning. You may need to add a pinch of salt
if you have used fresh or frozen onions.

Note: The canned small onions must be rinsed well to remove the
brine. Look for the M'lord brand. It is a product of Israel but seems to
be shipped all over North America. Use small fresh or frozen ones if
available.

Each serving provides:			
438	Calories	14 g	Carbohydrate
52 g	Protein	235 mg	Sodium
15 g	Total fat	136 mg	Cholesterol

Cajun Pot Roast

This is a modern-day version of an old-fashioned pot roast. If you are unable to find Cajun spice in your supermarket, we give a recipe below for making your own. You will find other uses for this seasoning as well. Try as a coating for poultry or fish before barbecuing. It will also add a little zing to your soups and a little zap to your salad dressings.

Makes 6 to 8 servings

Pot Roast

4	to 4¹/₂ pounds cross rib roast (some are leaner than others; pick a lean one)
4	teaspoons packaged Cajun spice (or use recipe following)
2	teaspoons olive oil
1	medium onion, chopped (about 1¹/₂ cups)
1	medium to large carrot, chopped (about 1 cup)
1	large clove garlic, minced
1	can (14 ounces) diced tomatoes
1	can (10 ounces) beef stock or homemade beef stock
2	tablespoons Dijon mustard
¹/₂	teaspoon thyme
¹/₄	teaspoon oregano
¹/₃	teaspoon Tabasco
6	small to medium potatoes, halved or quartered
6	carrots, halved crosswise
6	small onions, peeled

Cajun Spice

1	tablespoon paprika
³/₄	teaspoon cayenne pepper
¹/₂	teaspoon each white pepper, black pepper, dry mustard, and garlic powder
¹/₄	teaspoon each oregano and thyme
1	bay leaf finely crumbled

Coat surface of meat liberally on both sides with Cajun spice so most will adhere to beef. (If you're making your own Cajun spice, mix ingredients together and store any leftovers in a dry place.)

Heat olive oil in a Dutch oven and brown meat well on both sides over medium heat, about 5 minutes per side. Remove meat and set aside. Add onion and carrot to the pan and cook, stirring often (or giving pan a good shake) until onion starts to soften, about 2 minutes. Add garlic and cook for an additional 2 minutes (don't let garlic brown).

Return meat to the pan, placing it on top of the sautéed vegetables. Add tomatoes. Combine beef broth with Dijon mustard (best to mix mustard with a small amount of the broth first), then add thyme, oregano, and Tabasco. Pour around roast and vegetables. Bring to a boil; immediately reduce heat to simmer and cook for 2 hours, turning roast every 30 minutes.

Add the potatoes, carrots, and whole onions. Cook for an additional 45 minutes or until meat and vegetables are tender.

Remove meat and vegetables to a heated platter. Tip pan and skim off any fat and discard. Pour remaining juices into food processor or food mill and puree until smooth. Slice roast and arrange on serving platter; surround with vegetables. Pour gravy into a sauceboat and pass separately.

Each serving provides:			
496	Calories	40 g	Carbohydrate
53 g	Protein	591 mg	Sodium
14 g	Total fat	136 mg	Cholesterol

Brandied Pepper Steaks

From "chef David" comes the following recipe. He recommends decanting a bottle of your favorite red wine; while it is breathing, use the bottom of the bottle to pound the steaks.

This is a relatively quick and easy dinner for two. Serve with baked potato and broccoli or green salad.

Makes 2 servings

2	individual round steaks, trimmed of all visible fat
1¹/₂	tablespoons crushed black peppercorns
2	teaspoons olive oil
2	tablespoons brandy
1	tablespoon dried parsley
1	tablespoon liquid Bovril or instant beef stock
¹/₄	cup non-fat sour cream or lowfat plain yogurt

Pound steaks well with meat mallet (or bottom of wine bottle); this is important, as you need to break down the fibers in this lean, compact cut of beef. Work the crushed peppercorns into both sides of steaks with the heel of your hand. Let rest for about 1 hour.

Heat the olive oil in a small, heavy nonstick skillet over high heat and quickly sear the steaks on both sides. Continue to cook to desired doneness. Remove from pan and keep warm.

Stir brandy and parsley into the skillet and bring to a boil, scraping the skillet. Reduce heat, then add Bovril and sour cream and stir until smooth. Spoon over steaks and serve.

Each serving provides:

337	Calories	8 g	Carbohydrate
43 g	Protein	806 mg	Sodium
12 g	Total fat	96 mg	Cholesterol

Marilyn's Tenderloin Steaks

Prepare this dish, and with the right two people, you have the makings for a memorable evening. Serve with garlic mashed potatoes (page 241) or a mix of lightly sautéed mushrooms and diced red pepper added to wild rice, a Caesar salad with our reduced-fat Caesar dressing and homemade croutons (page 252) or a spinach salad (page 254), and crisply cooked fresh asparagus.

Makes 2 servings

2	tenderloin steaks, 1 inch to 1^1/$_2$ inches thick
^{2}/$_3$	cup dry red wine
1	teaspoon lite soy sauce
1	teaspoon Dijon mustard
2	teaspoons ketchup
2	teaspoons green or pink peppercorns (see note)

Preheat oven to 350°. Heat a small, heavy skillet over high heat and sear steaks quickly on both sides. Place meat in a shallow dish and bake for 7 to 10 minutes.

Meanwhile, wipe skillet, place over moderate heat, and pour in wine. Add soy sauce, Dijon mustard, ketchup, and peppercorns and bring to a boil. Reduce to a glaze-like or syrupy consistency. Spoon sauce over top of steaks and serve immediately (you only need about 1 to 2 tablespoons of this delicious, pungent sauce over each steak).

Note: Green or pink peppercorns are available in the gourmet section of many supermarkets. They are a bit pricey, but they last forever. In addition to the sauce in this recipe, we have a wonderful peppercorn sauce later in this chapter (see Trevor's New York Strip Loin Steaks with Three-Peppercorn Sauce on page 88). Between these two sauces, you no doubt will use the peppers up in no time.

Each serving provides:

314	Calories	2 g	Carbohydrate
41 g	Protein	358 mg	Sodium
14 g	Total fat	121 mg	Cholesterol

"Turf and a Bit of Surf" Party Steaks

Finishing the steaks in the oven gives you a last minute breather. This is a fairly expensive dish. You might want to scale it down for an intimate dinner for two. It would be perfect for Valentine's Day or an anniversary dinner. Serve with carrot bundles (page 235), fiddlehead greens, and wild rice.

Makes 4 servings

4	filet mignon steaks (6 to 8 ounces each), cut 1 inch to 1¹/₂ inches thick
2	to 4 ounces fresh crabmeat (enough to stuff in beef)
¹/₃	cup Grand Marnier
³/₄	cup mango chutney (cut up any large pieces)

Preheat oven to 350°. Make a pocket in the steaks by cutting horizontally through the center of the steaks, parallel to the surface of the meat, about ¹/₂ inch from each side. Cut to, but not through, the opposite side. Insert pieces of fresh crabmeat. Secure openings with toothpicks (break toothpicks in half so steaks will lie flat when searing).

Heat a heavy, ungreased skillet (cast-iron is best) over high heat and when very hot, sear steaks on both sides. Remove meat to a shallow casserole, leaving a little space between each steak. Bake for 7 minutes for 6-ounce steaks and 10 minutes for 8-ounce steaks. (Steaks will be medium rare.)

While steaks are baking, heat Grand Marnier in small saucepan; stir in chutney. When well blended and heated through, pour over steaks and serve.

Each serving provides:			
507	Calories	42 g	Carbohydrate
44 g	Protein	348 mg	Sodium
14 g	Total fat	134 mg	Cholesterol

Steak Diane

This dish is sophisticated, yet simple. Save the flaming-style versions for professionals!

Serve with baked potatoes and a medley of tiny (designer) vegetables if available or carrot bundles (page 235) and a puree of broccoli.

Makes 4 servings

2	tablespoons chopped fresh parsley
1	tablespoon Dijon mustard
2	teaspoons Worcestershire sauce
1	tablespoon olive oil
1	tablespoon butter or margarine
4	tenderloin steaks, 6 ounces each
1/2	cup chopped green onions
1/2	cup chopped fresh mushrooms (peel or brush, but don't wash)
1/2	cup dry vermouth
	salt and pepper to taste

Mix together the parsley, Dijon mustard, and Worcestershire sauce in a small dish or custard cup. Set aside.

Heat the oil and butter in a nonstick skillet over high heat and brown the steaks quickly. When they are cooked to the desired degree of doneness, remove to a warm platter. Add the green onions and mushrooms to the pan and sauté over medium heat until the onions are soft. Add the vermouth. Bring to a boil and cook for 2 minutes, stirring occasionally.

Stir in the mustard, Worcestershire sauce, and parsley mixture. Return to boiling while stirring constantly. As soon as sauce-like consistency is reached, pour over steaks immediately and serve.

	Each serving provides:		
399	Calories	3 g	Carbohydrate
41 g	Protein	205 mg	Sodium
21 g	Total fat	129 mg	Cholesterol

Todd's Steak Dijon

Serve this dish accompanied by wild rice and barely wilted spinach with diced and lightly sautéed red pepper, zucchini, and green onion.

Makes 4 servings

8	ounces non-fat sour cream
1	tablespoon Dijon mustard
1	tablespoon flour
4	eye of the round steaks, 4 ounces each, trimmed of all fat
1/2	teaspoon cracked black pepper
1	can (10 ounces) sliced mushrooms, drained
2	tablespoons red wine
1	tablespoon chopped chives or green onions

In a small bowl, whisk together the sour cream, Dijon mustard, and flour. Set aside.

Pound steaks well with a meat mallet to a 1/4-inch thickness. Sprinkle with the cracked pepper. Press pepper into steak with the heel of your hand and let sit for 1 hour at room temperature.

Spray a nonstick skillet with vegetable oil spray and brown steaks over medium heat, turning once to brown. Remove to a warm serving platter and keep warm.

Add mushrooms to the same skillet and sauté for 3 minutes. Add wine, stirring well. Stir in the sour cream, Dijon mustard, and flour mixture and bring to a boil. Cook for 1 minute, then pour over steaks. Top with chives and serve immediately.

Each serving provides:

281	Calories	8 g	Carbohydrate
31 g	Protein	399 mg	Sodium
13 g	Total fat	70 mg	Cholesterol

Beef Stroganoff

Because you are using an expensive and tender cut of beef, you want to end up with medium or medium rare strips of beef—so don't overcook. This dish seems wickedly rich, but it isn't!

Serve with cooked broad noodles or spaetzle, snow peas, and a green salad.

Makes 4 to 6 servings

1¼	pounds boneless top sirloin or beef tenderloin, trimmed of fat and cut at an angle into ¼-inch strips
2	teaspoons olive oil
½	pound fresh mushrooms, sliced
¼	cup dehydrated onion flakes
1	can (10 ounces) beef broth, undiluted
2	tablespoons tomato paste
1	tablespoon Worcestershire sauce
⅛	teaspoon garlic powder
⅛	teaspoon oregano
⅛	teaspoon freshly ground black pepper
	pinch of curry powder
2	tablespoons all-purpose flour
¼	cup sherry
½	to ¾ cup non-fat sour cream
2	to 3 tablespoons chopped fresh parsley

Brown beef quickly in large nonstick frying pan over high heat, to a medium-rare stage. Remove from pan.

Spray pan with nonstick cooking spray, add olive oil and sauté mushrooms until lightly browned. Stir in onion flakes, beef broth, tomato paste, Worcestershire sauce, garlic powder, oregano, pepper, and curry. Bring to a simmer.

Shake flour and sherry together in a small jar and stir into pan. Cook, stirring constantly until mixture starts to thicken. Stir in beef, sour cream, and parsley and heat thoroughly but do not boil.

Each serving provides:

260	Calories		10 g	Carbohydrate
29 g	Protein		313 mg	Sodium
9 g	Total fat		76 mg	Cholesterol

Minute Steaks Stuffed
with Wild Rice and Mushrooms

One of our testers remarked, "I would want this again, even if it wasn't lowfat!"
Serve with a julienne of carrots and parsnips (steamed and drizzled with a
tiny bit of maple syrup) and a tossed green salad.

Makes 4 servings

Steaks

1/2	cup wild rice
1/2	cup sliced mushrooms
1/4	cup diced water chestnuts
4	minute steaks, approximately 5 inches by 7 inches each
	garlic powder to taste
1	teaspoon beef bouillon granules

Mushroom Sauce

1/2	cup sliced mushrooms
2	teaspoons butter
1/2	cup dry red wine
	liquid saved from beef rolls (about 3/4 cup)
1	tablespoon cornstarch
1	tablespoon lite soy sauce
1	tablespoon sugar (or 2 tablespoons red currant jelly)
1/4	teaspoon freshly ground black pepper

Cook the rice: wash rice 3 times in warm water. Using a tightly covered pot, place 1 cup wild rice in 2 1/4 cups salted water. Bring to a boil, then reduce heat and simmer for 45 minutes. Remove from heat and let stand for 30 minutes. Stir lightly with a fork.

Spray a small nonstick skillet with nonstick cooking spray. Lightly sauté mushrooms over medium heat. Combine cooked rice, mushrooms, and water chestnuts.

Lay steaks flat on a working surface and sprinkle lightly with garlic powder. Divide rice-mushroom mixture evenly on top of steaks, spreading to cover surface of beef. Roll up each steak, jelly roll-fashion, and fasten with toothpicks. Secure ends with toothpicks to make sure filling does not spill out.

Spray a large nonstick skillet with nonstick cooking spray and brown the beef rolls on all sides over moderately high heat. Dissolve beef granules in ³/₄ cup water and pour into bottom of skillet. Cover and simmer until meat is tender, about 30 minutes.

To make the mushroom sauce, spray a nonstick skillet with non-stick cooking spray. Add mushrooms and butter. Sauté mushrooms, then add red wine. Bring to a boil. Stir in liquid from beef rolls (about ³/₄ cup). Dissolve cornstarch in soy sauce and stir into pan. Boil, stirring constantly, until thickened. Stir in sugar and black pepper.

Pour mushroom sauce over cooked beef rolls and serve at once (remove toothpicks before serving).

Note: Unused water chestnuts can be drained, placed in a jar, covered with cold water, and stored in the refrigerator. Change water daily.

Each serving provides:

317	Calories	24 g	Carbohydrate
29 g	Protein	461 mg	Sodium
10 g	Total fat	74 mg	Cholesterol

Rolled Stuffed Flank Steak (Braccioles)

If the name "braccioles" doesn't tell you that this is an Italian dish, the ingredients will: olive oil, garlic, Parmesan cheese, and tomato. When making the tomato sauce, don't leave any of the spices out if you want your dish to be as good as ours. As one of our testers exclaimed, "This isn't good, this is GREAT."

Serve with your choice of pasta, salad, and crusty buns. Any leftover cold meat makes wonderful sandwiches.

Makes 4 servings

Tomato Sauce

1	can (7^1/$_2$ ounces) tomato sauce
1	can (5^1/$_2$ ounces) tomato paste plus 2 cans water
2	tablespoons chopped fresh parsley
2	tablespoons sugar
^{1}/$_8$	teaspoon each dried basil, dried crushed red pepper, mint, and oregano

Steak

1^1/$_2$	pounds flank steak
2	cloves garlic, minced
^{1}/$_4$	cup chopped fresh parsley
^{1}/$_4$	cup freshly grated Parmesan cheese
^{1}/$_2$	teaspoon salt
^{1}/$_8$	teaspoon freshly ground black pepper
1^1/$_2$	tablespoons olive oil

Make the tomato sauce: place tomato sauce, tomato paste, and water in a 3-quart saucepan and bring to a boil. Reduce heat and simmer, covered, for 25 minutes, stirring occasionally. Add parsley, sugar, and spices and simmer for an additional 20 minutes.

Lay meat on a flat smooth working surface and flatten to a ^{1}/$_2$-inch thickness, pounding it lightly on both sides with the dull edge of a meat cleaver or a meat mallet. Keep the flank steak in one piece.

Cover steak with the garlic, parsley, Parmesan cheese, salt, and pepper. Roll steak up, jelly roll-fashion, and tie securely with cotton string. Secure ends with toothpicks.

Heat olive oil in a large, heavy nonstick skillet (that has a cover) over medium heat and brown the meat thoroughly on all sides, using tongs to turn so you don't puncture meat and let valuable juices escape. Don't rush this step—it should take at least 10 minutes.

Pour tomato sauce over meat, cover skillet, and simmer meat for about 1 hour or until tender. Do not overcook, or it will fall apart.

Each serving provides:

477	Calories	20 g	Carbohydrate
43 g	Protein	1191 mg	Sodium
25 g	Total fat	103 mg	Cholesterol

Beer Steak and Onions (Beef Carbonade)

Don't let this dish boil. A gentle simmer will produce tender meat in a flavor-ful sauce (actually, it is more a juice than a sauce). Broad noodles are the per-fect accompaniment to this Belgian dish. Steamed carrots complete the meal.

Makes 6 servings

1	tablespoon olive oil
2	pounds lean chuck steak, trimmed of all fat and sinew, and cut into individual portions
1	tablespoon unsalted butter
4	medium-large size onions, sliced
1	can or bottle (12 ounces) regular or dark beer
1	tablespoon brown sugar
$1/2$	teaspoon black pepper
2	bay leaves
2	tablespoons red wine vinegar
1	can (10 ounces) beef broth, undiluted
2	tablespoons minced fresh parsley

In a nonstick electric frying pan or heavy-bottomed skillet with lid, heat oil and brown steak on both sides. Remove from pan.

To the same pan, add butter and slowly cook onions over low to medium heat, stirring frequently, until tender and caramelized but not burned. This will take roughly 15 minutes—don't rush it! Remove onions to a bowl.

Stir beer into pan, scraping bottom, then add sugar, pepper, bay leaves, vinegar, and beef broth. Bring to a boil. Return steak to pan and cover meat well with onions. Simmer, covered tightly, until meat is tender, about 2 hours. Remove bay leaves and sprinkle with parsley before serving.

Each serving provides:

273	Calories	4 g	Carbohydrate
35 g	Protein	368 mg	Sodium
12 g	Total fat	96 mg	Cholesterol

Stuffed Minute-Steak Rolls

Serve this dish with mashed potatoes or noodles and green beans.

Makes 6 servings

1	cup coarsely crumbled, fresh whole wheat bread crumbs
1/2	teaspoon salt
1/8	teaspoon pepper
1/2	teaspoon caraway seeds
1/2	cup finely chopped onion
1	egg, slightly beaten
6	minute steaks (4 to 6 ounces each)
1	tablespoon butter or margarine
1	tablespoon olive oil
2	tablespoons Bisto (see note)
3/4	cup non-fat sour cream

Toss bread crumbs with salt, pepper, caraway seeds, and onion. Lightly stir in beaten egg to moisten.

Lay steaks flat on working surface and divide bread crumb–egg mixture evenly on top of each steak. Roll up each steak, jelly roll-fashion, and fasten with toothpicks.

Heat butter and olive oil in a heavy frying pan with lid over moderately high heat and brown meat rolls on all sides. Add 1 cup water and simmer, covered, until meat is tender, about 1 hour. Lift meat rolls onto a heated platter and keep warm.

Blend Bisto with 2 tablespoons cold water and stir into pan juices. Simmer 1 minute, stirring constantly. Stir in the sour cream and re-heat just to boiling point, but do not boil. Pour over meat rolls and serve.

Note: Bisto is a gravy maker, a product of the Campbell Soup Co.

Each serving provides:

270	Calories	9 g	Carbohydrate
29 g	Protein	575 mg	Sodium
13 g	Total fat	110 mg	Cholesterol

Eye of the Round Steaks with Mushrooms

Eye of the round steaks, unless marinated, could be a little on the tough side. However, if you follow our instructions, you will end up with steaks that are rare and juicy. Don't overcook! If you want a thick, juicy steak, you had better splurge on tenderloin or strip loin. We offer a choice of two different mushroom recipes to accompany the steaks. Don't overcook the mushrooms (people tend to forget that mushrooms can be eaten raw).

Serve with baked potatoes and Caesar salad (page 252).

Makes 2 servings

Steaks

2	eye of the round steaks (make sure it is the eye cut), 6 ounces each
$1/8$	teaspoon garlic powder
1	tablespoon butter or margarine

Mushrooms #1

1	tablespoon butter or margarine
1	tablespoon canola oil
$1/4$	pound small mushrooms, cut in half or quarters
2	shallots, finely chopped
$1/4$	cup dry vermouth

Mushrooms #2

$1/4$	pound small mushrooms, cut in half or quarters
1	tablespoon butter or margarine
1	clove garlic, minced
1	to 2 tablespoons teriyaki sauce

Freeze steaks partially, just until ice crystals begin to form. Remove any visible fat. Slice each steak horizontally into 2 thin slices. Place steaks between pieces of plastic wrap and, using the flat side of a meat mallet, pound them until they are about $1/4$-inch thick. Don't be afraid to give them a good whacking. They need to be pounded to almost twice their original size. Sprinkle both sides lightly with garlic powder. Melt butter in a heavy skillet over high heat and brown steaks very quickly on both sides. Don't overcook, they are best rare or medium rare. Place on a warm platter.

To make mushrooms #1, heat butter and oil in the same pan used to cook steaks. Brown mushrooms lightly, shaking the pan to turn mushrooms. Add shallots and vermouth. Cook, stirring, over high heat until most of the vermouth has evaporated.

To make mushrooms #2, lightly brown mushrooms in butter over medium heat, shaking pan to turn mushrooms. Add garlic and cook only until garlic is soft. Stir in the teriyaki sauce until well heated through.

Spoon mushrooms over the top of the steaks and serve immediately.

Note: Try to avoid buying prepackaged mushrooms. Select your own and choose firm, fresh mushrooms with tightly closed bottoms. Brush to clean or peel if necessary. If you need to store mushrooms for 3 to 4 days, use a brown paper bag, but if you need to store for a longer period, use a plastic container with holes punched in the lid (a large empty margarine tub will work; use a skewer to punch holes in the lid). Line the plastic container with paper towels, place a layer of mushrooms, another layer of paper towels, more mushrooms, etc. Mushrooms should keep this way for up to two weeks.

Mushrooms #1

Each serving provides:

540	Calories	6 g	Carbohydrate
41 g	Protein	214 mg	Sodium
38 g	Total fat	137 mg	Cholesterol

Mushrooms #2

Each serving provides:

464	Calories	5 g	Carbohydrate
41 g	Protein	557 mg	Sodium
31 g	Total fat	137 mg	Cholesterol

Trevor's New York Strip Loin Steaks with Three-Peppercorn Sauce

The Explorer Hotel in Yellowknife, Northwest Territories, serves a terrific steak with peppercorn sauce. The chef was kind enough to share the recipe with husband Trevor, but unfortunately it was a little too rich for this book (actually, a lot too rich). After some experimenting, the following sauce emerged and is really quite delicious. There is enough sauce for two large strip loins or four small or medium tenderloin steaks.

Serve with hash brown potatoes (page 243), baked cherry tomatoes (page 246) or tomatoes with chopped mushroom filling (page 247), and a spinach salad (page 254).

Makes 2 servings

Three-Peppercorn Sauce

2	teaspoons olive oil
2	tablespoons finely chopped shallots
1	tablespoon green peppercorns
1	tablespoon pink peppercorns
1	teaspoon cracked black peppercorns
4	tablespoons port (2-ounce bottles are available at liquor stores)
2	teaspoons liquid Bovril or instant beef stock
1	tablespoon tomato paste
3/4	cup 2 percent canned evaporated milk

Steaks

2	teaspoons butter or margarine
1	teaspoon safflower oil or canola oil
2	New York strip loins, 8 ounces each, trimmed of all visible fat

To make the peppercorn sauce, heat olive oil in a small, heavy-bottom nonstick skillet over medium heat and sauté shallots and peppercorns for 2 minutes to release the flavor. Shake pan a few times to turn the peppercorns evenly. Add port, increase heat to high, and cook until reduced to roughly half its original volume. Stir in the Bovril, then the tomato paste. Gradually stir in the milk. Simmer for 5 to 7 minutes or until sauce-like in consistency (it won't get thick—you want it to "nap" the steaks). Cover the sauce while you cook the steaks.

Heat butter or margarine and oil in a heavy skillet and cook steak over high heat for about 3 minutes on each side (for rare). Alternatively, steaks may be barbecued. Spoon sauce over steaks. Serve immediately.

Note: Green and pink peppercorns are much milder than black (see note for Marilyn's Tenderloin Steaks in this chapter). To crack peppercorns, put in a small bag and whack with the flat side of a meat mallet.

Each serving provides:

616	Calories	18 g	Carbohydrate
63 g	Protein	911 mg	Sodium
29 g	Total fat	173 mg	Cholesterol

Sauerbraten with Gingersnap Gravy

This meat has to be marinated for 4 or 5 days, so you must plan your meal ahead. The gingersnap gravy makes this dish. The sweetness of the gingersnaps balances the slightly sour flavor of the roast.

Serve with creamy mashed potatoes or potato dumplings, green beans, and diced turnips.

Makes 8 servings

Sauerbraten

4	to 5 pounds boneless rump roast
2	medium onions, sliced
1	carrot, diced
1	celery rib, diced
2	cups red wine vinegar
1/4	cup brown sugar, firmly packed
5	whole cloves
1/2	teaspoon whole peppercorns
1/4	teaspoon ground ginger
2	bay leaves
2	tablespoons flour
2	tablespoons canola oil or safflower oil

Gingersnap Gravy

1 1/2	cups juices from cooked meat (any fat skimmed off top)
2	tablespoons sugar
1/2	cup gingersnap crumbs (about 12 cookies)

Place meat in a glass bowl or other nonmetal container. Add vegetables. Combine vinegar, 2 cups water, and brown sugar and stir until sugar is dissolved. Add cloves, peppercorns, ground ginger, and bay leaves and pour over meat and vegetables. Cover and let stand in the refrigerator for 4 to 5 days, turning meat twice a day.

Remove meat, reserving marinade. Pat meat dry with paper towels, then dredge in flour.

Heat oil in Dutch oven and brown roast slowly on all sides. Drain off any fat. Strain marinade liquid and pour 2 cups over browned meat. Bring to a boil and immediately reduce heat. Simmer, covered tightly, for 2¹/2 to 3 hours until meat is tender; adding more marinade if necessary. Remove meat to a warm platter and keep warm.

To make the gravy, put 1¹/2 cups of the roast juices that have collected in the Dutch oven into a skillet; add ¹/2 cup water and the sugar. Bring to a boil, stirring to dissolve sugar. Stir in gingersnap crumbs and simmer until gravy thickens. Serve over sliced roast.

Each serving provides:

458	Calories	23 g	Carbohydrate
50 g	Protein	208 mg	Sodium
17 g	Total fat	136 mg	Cholesterol

Corned Beef 'n Cabbage Dinner

On March 17 (St. Patrick's Day), this might be considered a gourmet dinner. Choose a lean beef—briskets vary considerably in fat content. And don't forget to serve this dish with hot mustard!

Cooked and peeled whole potatoes and carrots plus slices of turnip complete the meal. These can be cooked separately but are really best cooked in the beef broth. If your pot isn't large enough to accommodate them, remove the cooked beef (cover to keep warm), and add the vegetables 15 minutes before adding the cabbage.

Makes 8 servings

3	tablespoons salt
3	tablespoons black pepper
1¹/₂	tablespoons powdered ginger
1¹/₂	teaspoons saltpeter (available at pharmacies)
4	pounds rolled brisket of beef, lean
4	cloves garlic, peeled
1	medium cabbage, cut into wedges

Combine salt, pepper, ginger, and saltpeter. Rub this mixture on all sides of the brisket. Put meat in a crock, enamel pot, or large glass dish (we use a punch bowl). Add cold water to cover the meat, and add the garlic. Place in the refrigerator or a cold place for 10 to 14 days.

Remove meat to a large pot or Dutch oven along with the brine. Do not add the sediment that will have settled in the bottom of the crock. You may have to add additional cold water to the pot to cover the meat. Bring to a boil (remove scum that forms), then reduce heat to simmer and cook for 3¹/₂ to 4 hours, or until the center of the beef can be pierced easily with a fork.

Skim any fat from the surface of the broth. Add cabbage during the last 15 to 20 minutes of cooking.

Note: We tie thread around the cabbage wedges before putting them in the pot to keep them tidy. You don't want bits of cabbage floating all over the pot.

	Each serving provides:		
413	Calories	9 g	Carbohydrate
55 g	Protein	2745 mg	Sodium
17 g	Total fat	162 mg	Cholesterol

Maria's "Slow, Slow, Slow" Sliced Beef

Last year we attended a buffet dinner party. One of the dishes was prepared by a wonderful woman from Portugal who spoke very little English. We were halfway into this book and, as this meat was the most tender imaginable, we asked Maria how she made it. The reply was "slow, slow, slow." This is how we now refer to this dish!

Makes 8 to 16 servings

3	to 6 pounds boneless sirloin tip roast
4	cloves garlic, minced
2	tablespoons pickled red bell pepper, minced (see note)
1	teaspoon cayenne pepper
$1/2$	teaspoon black pepper
$1/4$	teaspoon hot pepper flakes, optional
1	can (14 ounces) tomato sauce
$1/2$	teaspoon barbecue salt, or to taste
1	cup beer or red wine or white wine
2	tablespoons vegetable oil

Slice beef into serving-size portions, roughly $1/4$ inch thick. Tenderize, using a meat mallet.

Combine garlic, pickled pepper, cayenne, black, and hot pepper, tomato sauce, barbecue salt, and beer and pour over meat. Let marinate for a minimum of 4 hours.

Remove meat from marinade and blot dry. Heat vegetable oil in a large electric skillet over medium-high heat and cook beef slices, turning occasionally, until almost cooked; test with a fork.

When beef is almost cooked, pour the entire marinade over meat and simmer, covered, until beef is cooked very tender and marinade is reduced to a thick, gravy-like consistency. This will take about 1 hour.

Note: Pickled red bell peppers, if not available at your local supermarket, can be found at Italian or Portuguese food stores.

	Each serving provides:		
281	Calories	2 g	Carbohydrate
42 g	Protein	205 mg	Sodium
10 g	Total fat	117 mg	Cholesterol

Oven

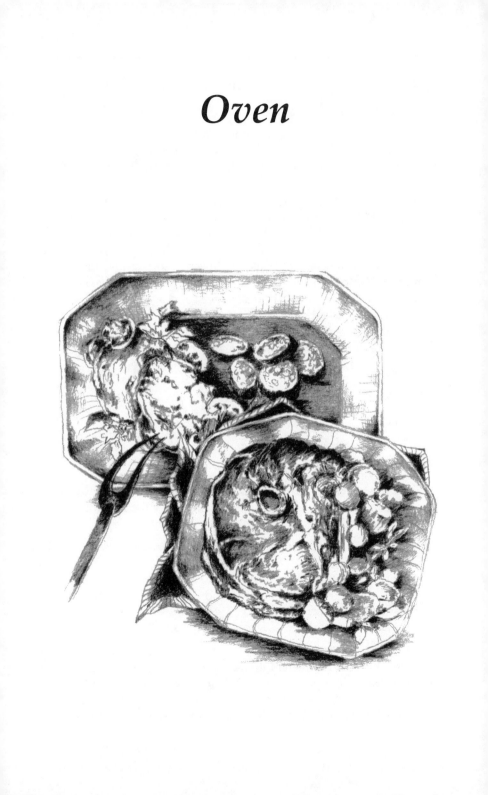

Here are just a few hints we would like to pass along regarding cooking beef in the oven:

- Try browning stew meat and ground meat under the broiler rather than in a frying pan. This will allow fat to drip away.
- Roast meat on a rack so that the fat drips off and can be discarded.
- Use a nonstick cooking spray for greasing baking dishes and baking pans. These sprays are made from a natural substance called lecithin, and they do a very good job of preventing sticking.
- Always trim all visible fat from meat *before* cooking.
- Fresh meat should be refrigerated or frozen as soon as possible after purchasing. Warm or even room temperatures promote the growth of microorganisms and also speed spoilage.
- For perfectly cooked steaks (tenderloin, lean rib eye, and New York strip loin), see our introduction to the "Stove-Top" chapter. These steaks are started on top of the stove but are finished in the oven.

Roasting

Following are general tips for roasting various cuts of beef.

Round, Rump, and Sirloin Tip

Place roast, fat side up, on a rack in a roasting pan. Do not cover. Season to taste, but do not use salt, as this will dry the meat on top. Try one of the following:

- Rub roast with garlic clove or 1 teaspoon garlic powder and cracked black pepper.
- Mix 2 tablespoons Dijon mustard with 1 tablespoon lemon juice, 1 tablespoon cracked peppercorns, and 1/2 teaspoon dried oregano (this is Clark's favorite).
- Make an herb rub: mix 1 tablespoon thyme and 1 teaspoon each of rosemary, sage, and pepper.

Insert a meat thermometer into the center of the roast, avoiding fat and bone. Roast in a preheated 500° oven for 30 minutes. Add 1 cup water, reduce oven temperature to 275°, and roast until the meat thermometer registers 155°. This will produce medium doneness.

Roasting time at 275° will range from 1¹/₄ to 1³/₄ hours for a 2-pound to 5-pound roast (eye of the round roasts, because of their shape, usually take only 60 minutes, so check your thermometer).

Remove roast from oven and let sit covered with foil for 15 minutes before carving. Internal temperature will rise approximately 5°.

This cooking method is not recommended for roasting past medium doneness.

Rib, Tenderloin, and Sirloin (Not Sirloin Tip)

These directions are for the more tender cuts. Place the roast fat side up on rack in roasting pan without lid. Season to taste. Insert a meat thermometer into the center of the roast, avoiding fat or bone. Cook as follows in a preheated 325° oven. Rare: 20 minutes per pound; medium: 25 minutes per pound; well done: 30 minutes per pound.

Do not add any liquid to the pan during roasting time.

To make a lowfat gravy: skim any fat in roasting pan with a spoon or bulb baster. (Kitchen specialty shops have specially designed pitchers with spouts starting at the bottom for separating the fat (on top) from the juice (on the bottom), and they work!) Another method is to drop ice cubes into strained drippings; this chills the fat, which adheres to the ice cube and can be discarded with the ice.

Combine 4 tablespoons flour with 4 tablespoons water and stir into the defatted drippings in roasting pan. Turn heat to medium and slowly stir in 2 cups beef stock, or 2 cups boiling water to which 2 beef bouillon cubes have been crumbled. Cook, stirring constantly, until thickened. Season to taste. Dried thyme (¹/₄ teaspoon) is a good addition, and try stirring in 2 tablespoons red currant jelly occasionally, for a little added interest.

Standing Prime Rib Roast

Standing prime rib roast and rib eye roasts really don't belong in a lowfat gourmet beef cookbook; on the other hand, we don't feel a beef cookbook would be complete if it didn't include the "king" and "queen" of roasts. Insert slivers of garlic into fat in both these roasts and sprinkle with seasoned salt before cooking. It is important that both these roasts be at room temperature before cooking, for accurate timing.

Preheat oven to 350° for 5 minutes (this means 5 minutes after indicator light goes off). Place roast in roasting pan and roast, uncovered, for exactly 1 hour. Turn oven off. Do not open oven door!

Roast should be in the oven for at least 2 hours. Forty-five minutes before serving, turn oven back on to 325° and cook for 45 minutes. Roast will be medium rare. Instead of Yorkshire pudding, substitute Louise's Popovers (see page 234).

A friend of ours cuts away that considerably large-sized V-shaped piece of fat found in prime rib roasts and inserts the end slices from a loaf of bread. This bread absorbs some of the remaining fat when it is cooking. The crusts are then discarded before the roast is carved. This method can be used with turkeys or large roasting chickens as well to reduce the amount of fat leached into the dressing; the end crust of bread is placed over the stuffing at the opening of the cavity just before it is skewered or sewn closed.

Each 6 oz. serving provides:

402	Calories	0 g	Carbohydrate
47 g	Protein	124 mg	Sodium
22 g	Total fat	138 mg	Cholesterol

Rib Eye Roast

For a 5- to 6-pound rib eye roast, preheat oven to 500° for 5 minutes. Cook meat for 20 minutes, uncovered. Turn oven to lowest setting (140°) for 8 hours. Do not open oven door during this time! Remove roast from oven and let sit for 10 minutes before carving. Roast will be medium rare.

Each 6 oz. serving provides:

376	Calories	0 g	Carbohydrate
48 g	Protein	116 mg	Sodium
19 g	Total fat	136 mg	Cholesterol

Onion-Smothered Pot Roast

Question: Why do you take the cover off after an hour, bake for another hour, and put the cover back on for another hour? Answer: Because Mother always did it that way! This reminds us of the story of a gal who always had the butcher cut the shank end off a ham before she cooked it. When questioned, she explained that her mother always did this. When the mother was questioned, it was because her mother always did this. It turns out that Granny never had a pan large enough to accommodate a whole ham!

Mashed potatoes are an absolute must with this roast. If you have been good and cut off all the visible fat, you will end up with delicious fat-free pan juices, laden with onions. Spoon this over the sliced meat. Mashed turnips and green peas round out the meal. Don't forget the horseradish!

Makes 6 to 8 servings

4	to 5 pounds top or bottom round roast, room temperature
2	teaspoons lite soy sauce
4	cloves garlic, minced
	freshly ground pepper
1	teaspoon paprika
2	to 3 large onions, thinly sliced

Preheat oven to 350°. With a sharp knife, remove all visible fat from roast. Rub both sides of meat first with soy sauce, then with garlic. Sprinkle with pepper and paprika. Place in a small roasting pan that has a tight-fitting lid. Cover well with onions. Bake, covered, for 1 hour. Remove cover and bake for 1 hour uncovered. Replace cover and bake for 1 additional hour.

Each serving provides:

379	Calories	7 g	Carbohydrate
51 g	Protein	286 mg	Sodium
14 g	Total fat	136 mg	Cholesterol

Marinated Rump Roast

Makes 6 servings

4	pounds rump roast
1	large onion, thinly sliced
1	large carrot, thinly sliced
1¹/₂	cups red wine
¹/₂	teaspoon basil
¹/₂	teaspoon thyme
2	tablespoons brown sugar
2	tablespoons flour
¹/₂	teaspoon salt or salt substitute
1	tablespoon chili sauce
¹/₂	cup orange juice

Place roast in a deep glass or stainless steel bowl and top with the onion, carrot, wine, basil, and thyme. Cover and marinate overnight in the refrigerator, turning occasionally. (A heavy zip-lock plastic bag is also good for marinating.) Remove from the refrigerator 1 hour before cooking.

Preheat the broiler. Remove meat from marinade (save marinade) and pat dry with paper towel. Place in a small roasting pan. Sprinkle top surface with 1 tablespoon brown sugar and place under broiler until brown sugar melts and is glazed, about 3 to 4 minutes. Turn roast over and repeat this procedure, using the remaining 1 table-spoon brown sugar.

Preheat oven to 325°. Place marinade in medium saucepan and bring to a boil. Shake flour, salt, chili sauce, and orange juice together in a small jar and stir into hot marinade. Cook until slightly thickened. Spoon hot marinade mixture over top and around meat, cover tightly, and bake for 3 hours, or until tender.

Each serving provides:			
645	Calories	15 g	Carbohydrate
72 g	Protein	380 mg	Sodium
30 g	Total fat	240 mg	Cholesterol

Indoor Barbecued Roast

You don't need a barbecue to achieve a wonderfully delicious smoky barbecue flavor. Serve with mashed potatoes, carrots, and green beans or broccoli.

Makes 6 to 8 servings

4	to 6 pounds top or bottom round roast, or rump
	garlic powder
	paprika
1/2	cup Liquid Smoke (found in many supermarkets)
2	medium onions, chopped
	Worcestershire sauce, for sprinkling on top of roast
3/4	cup barbecue sauce
2	tablespoons cornstarch
3	tablespoons dry red wine

Sprinkle roast on both sides with garlic powder and paprika. Pour Liquid Smoke over top and cover with chopped onion. Place meat in a zip-lock freezer bag to marinate. Refrigerate overnight.

Preheat oven to 275°. At cooking time, drain Liquid Smoke and discard. Sprinkle roast liberally with Worcestershire sauce. Cover with foil and bake for 5 hours. Uncover, pour barbecue sauce over the meat and bake for 1 additional hour. Remove roast to a warm platter (save the pan juices).

Dissolve cornstarch in red wine and stir into pan juices. Let boil, stirring constantly, until the liquid reaches a sauce-like consistency. Serve sauce separately in a sauceboat.

	Each serving provides:		
393	Calories	11 g	Carbohydrate
50 g	Protein	381 mg	Sodium
14 g	Total fat	136 mg	Cholesterol

Dad's Plank Steak

This was Dad's specialty and it was saved for special dinners at weekends in the country. Mother picked up the steak at the butchers, made the mashed potatoes, prepared glazed carrots and fresh peas, and baked a fresh berry pie, but this was always referred to as Dad's specialty. Mind you, Dad was the one who ordered the plank from the lumberyard (although Mom seasoned it). He actually ordered two: one has been out on loan to a friend for about 10 years, but nobody remembers who borrowed it!

Serve with fresh carrots and peas.

Makes 8 servings

3	pounds sirloin steak, 2 inches thick
1	clove garlic, cut in half
1	teaspoon dry mustard
1	teaspoon sugar
3	to 4 cups mashed potatoes

For this recipe you will need an oak plank that is 14 inches long, 2 inches thick, and at least 10 inches wide (see note).

Preheat broiler. Rub steak on both sides with garlic, then sprinkle with a mixture of dry mustard and sugar. Broil for 5 minutes on one side only.

Preheat the oven to 250°. Place browned side down in middle of plank and surround with a thick layer of mashed potatoes. The un-cooked side of the steak will be exposed on top. Surrounding the meat with the potatoes helps to seal off the juices that will be emitted during the cooking process, but in case there are any leaks, it is best to place the plank on a cookie sheet. Bake for 2 hours. Steak will be rare and tender. Slice vertically and serve with a portion of the mashed potatoes.

Note: The hardest part of this recipe is finding the plank, but once you have purchased the plank and have seasoned it, it will last for years. It is a really impressive dish to serve, and it's the perfect dish for the person who could just never master the art of barbecuing. Make sure you order a plank with the above specifications. Season the plank by rubbing it with vegetable oil and placing in a 300° oven. Turn oven off until cool. Do this 5 or 6 times, so it is permanently seasoned. It is worth the effort.

Each serving provides:

365	Calories	15 g	Carbohydrate
46 g	Protein	337 mg	Sodium
14 g	Total fat	131 mg	Cholesterol

Perfect Roast Filet of Beef

The filet of beef is the most succulent cut of beef there is and, therefore, the most expensive. A filet roast automatically adds a festive air to any meal, so great care must be taken with its preparation. Because it is so naturally tender and juicy, you want to enhance these qualities by cooking it to perfection. If you like well-done beef, go for a pot roast—don't spoil a filet by overcooking.

Serve with baked stuffed potatoes (page 240), fresh asparagus, and tomatoes with chopped mushroom filling (page 247).

Makes 5 to 6 servings

2	to $2^1/2$ pounds whole beef tenderloin roast
1	tablespoon soy sauce
$1/8$	teaspoon sugar

Trim any sinew and excess fat from roast. Brush meat all over with soy sauce then sprinkle lightly with sugar. Let sit for 1 hour at room temperature.

Preheat oven to 500°. When it has reached this temperature, wait 5 minutes before placing meat in oven. Bake 3 minutes for rare, 4 minutes for medium, and 5 minutes for well done.

As soon as the roast has cooked according to desired degree of doneness, turn the oven off without opening the door and leave the roast in the oven for 2 hours. Do not open the oven during this time.

Each serving provides:

201	Calories	0 g	Carbohydrate
28 g	Protein	236 mg	Sodium
9 g	Total fat	81 mg	Cholesterol

Cicely's Christmas Filet

This roast requires less time than the Perfect Roast Filet of Beef (see previous recipe). We call it Cicely's Christmas Filet because for years Cicely would call at Christmas time to ask "How do I cook that filet of beef?" For a festive touch, decorate the meat platter with clumps of parsley and tiny red Christmas ornaments (or cherry tomatoes).

Serve with duchesse potatoes, vegetable-stuffed red peppers (page 239), and spinach salad (page 254).

Makes 5 to 6 servings

2	tablespoons dry mustard
3	cloves garlic, minced
	lots of freshly ground black pepper
2	to 3 teaspoons olive oil
2	to 2¹/2 pounds tenderloin roast of beef, room temperature

Preheat oven to 450°. Make a paste with the mustard, garlic, pepper, and oil. Rub it all over the beef.

Place beef on a rack in a shallow roasting pan and place in center of oven. Immediately reduce oven temperature to 400°. Roast for 35 minutes. Meat will be rare and tender just the way a filet should be served. Let sit for 10 minutes before carving. This can be served hot, or it may be served cold at a buffet.

Each serving provides:

224	Calories	1 g	Carbohydrate
28 g	Protein	62 mg	Sodium
11 g	Total fat	81 mg	Cholesterol

Twenty-Four-Hour Roast

*If you want to prepare a large roast of beef for a crowd, you have to know
about this roast. Five years ago we would have recommended a rolled standing
rib roast or a rib eye roast, but the fat content is pretty high. A blade chuck
roast from the shoulder, which is a more muscled area of the beef, is leaner. It
is also tougher, but when it's cooked in the following manner, it becomes one
of the best roasts you will eat. However, you must use a blade chuck roast
with the bone in. It must not weigh less than 14 pounds nor more than 22
pounds.*

*Serve with mashed potatoes, green peas, baby carrots, and marinated
onions. Don't forget the horseradish! Not all of your guests will be on a fat-
restricted diet and for sure they will be looking for some gravy. Our best ad-
vice is to buy several packages of the commercial gravy mix and prepare as
directed (a mix seems to work well—be sure to include some demi-glace). Stir
in the juice from the roast, skimming off any surface fat.*

Makes 16 to 22 servings

14   to 22 pounds blade chuck roast, bone in

Preheat oven to 175°. Place roast in a large roasting pan. Do not
season, even with salt and pepper, and do not cover. Bake for 24
hours. Do not open oven door during this time!

Each serving provides:

426	Calories	0 g	Carbohydrate
53 g	Protein	120 mg	Sodium
22 g	Total fat	180 mg	Cholesterol

Herb-Roasted Eye of the Round Roast

Eye of the round roast is not as tender as a filet of beef, therefore, it is best to marinate this cut. However, if you have no time to marinate, you can use this recipe or, for more special occasions, the Eye of the Round Roast au Jus recipe that follows. You will be very pleased with the results. It is important, however, to slice the meat thinly across the grain when serving and not to cook it beyond the medium-rare stage (eye of the round roast is best served rare or medium rare). Also, it is important to have the meat at room temperature for accurate timing.

Serve with Louise's Popovers (page 234), lowfat roast potatoes (if you have two ovens), green peas, and parsnip and carrot puree (to make the puree, cook parsnips and carrots in the same pot, drain when tender, and mash with a dab of butter or margarine. If you like a fine puree, put it in the food processor).

Makes 5 to 6 servings

2	to 2¹/₂ pounds eye of the round roast, room temperature
2	teaspoons olive oil
1	teaspoon oregano
1	teaspoon paprika
¹/₂	teaspoon garlic powder
¹/₂	teaspoon black pepper

Preheat oven to 500°. Rub roast all over with oil. Combine oregano, paprika, garlic powder, and pepper and rub on both sides of meat. Place meat in baking pan and roast for 30 minutes. Then add 1 cup water, reduce temperature to 275°, and roast for an additional 45 minutes to 60 minutes, or until meat thermometer registers 155°. This will produce a medium doneness. Remove from oven and let sit covered with foil for 15 minutes before carving to allow juices to settle (internal temperature will rise 5°).

Each serving provides:

310	Calories	1 g	Carbohydrate
35 g	Protein	77 mg	Sodium
18 g	Total fat	92 mg	Cholesterol

Eye of the Round Roast au Jus

For serving suggestions, see the previous recipe for Herb-Roasted Eye of the Round Roast.

Cold roast beef makes great sandwiches the next day, especially when topped with very thinly sliced mild onion and spread with any leftover sauce.

Makes 8 to 10 servings

4	pounds eye of the round roast, trimmed of any visible fat
4	teaspoons dried basil
1	teaspoon freshly ground black pepper
1	large clove garlic, minced
1	tablespoon soy sauce
1/2	teaspoon sugar
1	tablespoon vegetable oil
2	medium carrots, diced
2	medium onions, diced
2	cups beef broth, homemade or low-salt canned (if you use canned, use 1 can plus 3/4 can of water)

Place roast in pan (a 9 × 13-inch pan works well). Make a paste of basil, pepper, garlic, soy sauce, sugar, and oil and rub all over meat. Let sit at room temperature for 1 hour.

Preheat oven to 500°. Add diced carrots and onions to pan. Bake for 30 minutes. Reduce oven temperature to 275° and roast for approximately 1 to 1 1/4 hours or until meat thermometer registers 155°. This cooks the meat to medium. Let the meat sit covered with foil while you make the jus (sauce).

To make the sauce, remove meat from the pan and pour off any fat. Add beef broth and stir, scraping anything that has adhered to the bottom of the pan. Pour this, along with the roasted carrots and onions, into a saucepan and simmer, mashing the vegetables into the liquid. Season to taste and strain into a gravy boat. For a slightly thicker sauce, place cooked vegetables plus a little pan juice into a food processor and puree; then stir into remaining juice. Serve over thinly sliced meat (make sure to carve across the grain).

Each serving provides:			
384	Calories	3 g	Carbohydrate
42 g	Protein	202 mg	Sodium
21 g	Total fat	112 mg	Cholesterol

Easy Barbecue for a Crowd

This is in the oven section rather than the barbecue section because the meat is cooked in the oven. When purchasing the meat, be sure to tell the butcher that you will be bringing it back the next day to be sliced. Butchers take pride in their work and are very accommodating.

When serving, have on hand an assortment of salads, including coleslaw, and some dill pickles.

Makes 24 to 30 servings

1   large sirloin tip roast (roughly 18 pounds)
1   quart barbecue sauce
     white and whole wheat buns

Bake the roast in a preheated, 325° oven until medium rare. This will take approximately 2 1/2 to 3 hours. Use a thermometer for accurate timing—140° for rare, 160° for medium, and 170° for well done.

Remove roast from oven and let stand for at least 1 hour. Wrap well in foil and return to butcher to be thinly sliced. Heat barbecue sauce in a saucepan and add meat until meat is reheated. Serve on buns.

Each serving provides:

392	Calories	13 g	Carbohydrate
56 g	Protein	446 mg	Sodium
11 g	Total fat	157 mg	Cholesterol

Marinated Eye of the Round Roast #1

When serving eye of the round roast, carve thinly across the grain. Do not cook beyond the medium-rare stage or it will not be tender.

Serve with potatoes, carrot and parsnip julienne (steam and drizzle with a tablespoon of maple syrup), and fresh broccoli.

Makes 6 to 8 servings

1/2   cup dry sherry
1/2   cup orange juice
1/4   cup lite soy sauce
2   tablespoons onion flakes
2   tablespoons brown sugar
2 1/2 to 3 pounds eye of the round roast

Combine sherry, orange juice, soy sauce, onion, and brown sugar. Marinate beef and place in refrigerator overnight. Turn meat occasionally.

Preheat oven to 325°. Remove meat from marinade (save the marinade) before placing in small roasting pan. Bake for 20 minutes per pound for rare and 25 minutes per pound for medium rare, basting occasionally with marinade.

Remaining marinade may be simmered in a small saucepan to reduce slightly, then spooned over the carved meat.

Each serving provides:			
322	Calories	7 g	Carbohydrate
33 g	Protein	375 mg	Sodium
15 g	Total fat	87 mg	Cholesterol

Marinated Eye of the Round Roast #2

This is sometimes referred to as a shell-bone roast. It is solid, lean meat and very easy to carve.

If you have any leftover red wine, it is a simple matter to make your own marinade. Use 3 parts wine to 1 part olive oil. Add garlic powder and lots of freshly ground black pepper. It won't be fat-free, but it will be cheaper!

For serving suggestions, see the previous recipe for Marinated Eye of the Round Roast #1.

Makes 6 servings

2¹/₂   pounds eye of the round roast
8   ounce bottle of fat-free Italian-style salad dressing

Marinate the roast in the dressing for 2 to 3 days, turning occasionally. Keep refrigerated. Bring roast to room temperature before cooking, for accurate timing.

Preheat oven to 325°. Bake for 20 minutes per pound for rare and 25 minutes per pound for medium rare. When serving, slice thinly across the grain.

Note: If you don't like figuring out times, here's a formula that works well. Roast the eye of the round at 350° for 1 hour for rare or at 400° for 1 hour for medium rare.

Each serving provides:			
372	Calories	0 g	Carbohydrate
43 g	Protein	208 mg	Sodium
21 g	Total fat	115 mg	Cholesterol

Beef Wellington

Here it is: a reduced-fat version of one of the most elegant entrées of all time.

Makes 5 to 6 servings

Beef Wellington

2	pounds beef tenderloin roast
3	tablespoons butter or margarine
$1/2$	pound fresh mushrooms, chopped fine
1	teaspoon flour
	salt, to taste
	freshly ground pepper, to taste
4	sheets filo pastry
2	tablespoons canola oil (use extra if needed for the brushing process)
3	tablespoons fine dry bread crumbs

Escargot Sauce

3	tablespoons butter or margarine
1	clove garlic, minced
4	green onions
1	tablespoon flour
1	tablespoon Bisto gravy mix (see note)
1	can (10 ounces) beef broth, undiluted
$3/4$	cup red wine
1	can ($4^{1}/2$ ounces) escargots, drained (cut any large escargots in half)

Preheat oven to 400°. Remove any muscle tissue and fat left on the beef, then place in an uncovered roasting pan. Roast 20 minutes for rare and 30 minutes for medium. Let cool. This precooking step is important, because once the beef is wrapped in pastry, it is in the oven only long enough to cook the pastry and heat the meat through. Reduce oven temperature to 375°.

Melt butter in a nonstick skillet, then add the mushrooms, flour, salt, and pepper. Stir for several minutes over medium heat. Let cool.

Unroll the filo pastry carefully. Using a corner, count out 4 sheets. Keep sheets covered with a damp cloth. Lay 1 sheet of filo pastry down on your work surface and lightly brush with oil, making sure to brush right to edges. Sprinkle with 1 tablespoon of the bread crumbs. Lay a second sheet directly over the first and again brush lightly with oil and sprinkle with crumbs. Lay a third sheet on top of the second and brush with oil and sprinkle with crumbs. Place fourth layer on top of third and brush with oil but do not sprinkle with crumbs.

Arrange cooked mushrooms in center of pastry and spread enough to make a bed for the beef. Place beef on top of the mushrooms and roll up in pastry, envelope-style. Spray a baking sheet with a nonstick cooking spray, then place pastry seam side down on the sheet. Bake for 25 minutes. Remove from oven and let stand for 15 minutes before placing on warmed serving platter. Carve in $3/4$-inch slices and accompany it with Escargot Sauce.

To make the sauce, melt butter in a small saucepan. Sauté garlic and onions. Sprinkle with flour, then add Bisto and blend in. Gradually add the broth and wine and cook, stirring constantly, until thickened. Stir in the escargots and simmer gently until escargots are well heated through.

Note: Return unused portion of filo to the refrigerator and use within two weeks. Bisto is a gravy maker produced by Campbell Soup Co.

Each serving provides:

483	Calories	15 g	Carbohydrate
38 g	Protein	787 mg	Sodium
29 g	Total fat	139 mg	Cholesterol

Southwest Sirloin Tip or Rump Roast with Chili Popovers

This roast is excellent when cooked on the rotisserie. Let roast stand at room temperature for 1 hour after seasoning. Cook over medium-hot coals or at medium setting on electric or gas barbecue. Allow 20 minutes per pound for rare or 25 minutes per pound for medium. (See page 96 for alternate seasonings for a sirloin tip or rump.)

Makes 8 to 10 servings

Roast

1	tablespoon prepared mustard
2	tablespoons brown sugar
1	tablespoon chili powder
1	teaspoon cumin
$1/2$	teaspoon no-salt seasoning (page 260)
$1/4$	teaspoon pepper
3	to 4 pounds sirloin tip or rump roast (can be larger)

Chili Popovers

3	eggs, room temperature
$1/2$	teaspoon salt
1	cup 2 percent milk
1	cup flour
$3/4$	teaspoon chili powder
$1/8$	teaspoon Tabasco

Combine mustard, brown sugar, chili powder, cumin, no-salt seasoning, and pepper. Spread on meat and let sit at room temperature for 1 hour.

Preheat oven to 500°. Place roast, fat side up, on a rack in a roasting pan. Do not cover. Insert meat thermometer into center of roast, avoiding fat and bone. Roast for 30 minutes. Add 1 cup water and reduce oven temperature to 275°. Roast until meat thermometer registers 155° to cook the meat to medium (this cooking method is not recommended for roasting past medium). Roasting time at 275° will range from $1 1/4$ to $1 3/4$ hours for a 2- to 5-pound roast.

Remove roast from oven and let sit covered with foil for 15 minutes before carving. Internal temperature will rise approximately 5°.

To make the popovers, spray Teflon muffin tins with nonstick cooking spray. Whisk eggs and salt lightly. Add milk, flour, chili powder, and Tabasco and mix just until blended. Don't overmix (it can be a little lumpy). Fill the tins halfway. Place into a cold oven. Turn oven on to 425° and bake for 20 minutes. Reduce oven temperature to 375° and bake for an additional 10 to 15 minutes or until the popovers are golden brown and crisp on top. Turn oven off. Pierce each popover with a skewer to release steam and let popovers sit in closed oven for an additional 2 to 3 minutes. Makes 8 popovers (giant muffin tins are available, or use custard cups for 6 large popovers).

	Each serving provides:		
299	Calories	15 g	Carbohydrate
37 g	Protein	243 mg	Sodium
9 g	Total fat	160 mg	Cholesterol

Busy Day Curry

This is one of those "walk away and forget about it" dishes we all like to have in our repertoire.

Serve with hot fluffy rice (Basmati rice is particularly nice with curries) and condiments of your choice, such as chutney, chopped bananas (sprinkled with a little lemon juice to prevent discoloration), chopped cooked egg white, chopped dry-roasted peanuts, and pappadams (see note). This is also delicious with Doreen's Special Salad (page 251).

Makes 4 to 6 servings

2	pounds lean stew beef, trimmed of any excess fat and sinew
2	stalks celery, chopped
2	onions, chopped
2	carrots, grated
1	teaspoon no-salt seasoning (page 260) or salt
2	tablespoons curry powder
1	tablespoon sugar
4	tablespoons instant tapioca
1	can (10 ounces) tomato juice
1	can (10 ounces) beef broth
2	to 3 tablespoons raisins
1	small green apple, chopped

Preheat oven to 250°. Combine all of the above ingredients in a shallow casserole. Cover tightly and bake for 4 hours.

Note: Pappadams (a type of Indian flatbread) are normally fried in hot oil, but if they make a curry dinner for you, try cooking them in the microwave without any oil. Place 4 small pappadams in the microwave oven and cook on high until they are puffed evenly. This will take about 3 minutes.

Each serving provides:			
349	Calories	27 g	Carbohydrate
37 g	Protein	677 mg	Sodium
10 g	Total fat	92 mg	Cholesterol

Easy Oven Stew

With this recipe, there's no need to brown the meat first—the appearance and flavor will not suffer by eliminating this step.

It's hard to imagine that this could taste any better than when served right away, but wait until you taste any leftovers the following day!

Makes 4 servings

1¹/₂ pounds lean stew meat, cut into 1-inch pieces and all visible fat removed
1 medium onion, cut into 1-inch pieces
2 large carrots, cut into 1-inch pieces
2 medium potatoes, cut into quarters
1 can (14 ounces) Italian-style plum tomatoes, or stewed tomatoes (break up any large pieces of tomato with a fork)
1¹/₄ cups beef broth
1 can (7¹/₂ ounces) tomato sauce
¹/₄ cup instant tapioca
1 teaspoon instant coffee granules
1 teaspoon no-salt seasoning (page 260) or salt
¹/₂ teaspoon thyme
2 tablespoons chopped fresh parsley, optional

Preheat oven to 250°. Combine all of the above ingredients, except parsley, in a shallow casserole. Cover tightly with lid or foil and bake for at least 4 hours. Serve sprinkled with chopped fresh parsley.

Each serving provides:			
434	Calories	41 g	Carbohydrate
42 g	Protein	1006 mg	Sodium
11 g	Total fat	102 mg	Cholesterol

Steak and Mushroom Pie

Both of our husbands are fond of steak and kidney pie, but because kidneys are very high in cholesterol, we decided to substitute small fresh mushrooms for the kidneys. One husband remarked "This is delicious!" The other husband (not to be outdone) said "I think it is better than delicious!"
Serve with whipped parsnips and green peas.

Makes 8 servings

2¹/2	pounds lean chuck beef, cut into 1-inch to 1¹/2-inch cubes

2¹/2   pounds lean chuck beef, cut into 1-inch to 1¹/2-inch cubes
1/2   cup plus 3 tablespoons whole wheat flour
1/2   plus 1/4 teaspoon paprika
1/4   teaspoon black pepper
2   tablespoons olive oil
1   pint small pearl onions, peeled (about 24)
1   pound mushrooms (leave small ones whole and cut larger ones into halves or quarters)
1   large clove garlic, minced
1¹/2   cups beef broth
1   cup dry red wine
2   tablespoons tomato paste
1   tablespoon Worcestershire sauce
1/2   teaspoon thyme
4   sheets filo pastry
2   tablespoons canola oil (use a bit extra if needed for the brushing process)
3   tablespoons fine dry bread crumbs

Preheat the broiler. Place the meat in a plastic bag to which you have added 1/2 cup of the flour, 1/4 teaspoon of the paprika, and pepper. Shake well until meat is coated. Place meat on a cookie sheet and brown under the broiler, about 5 minutes (one side only is fine). Set aside while you make the sauce. Reduce oven temperature to 300°.

Heat oil in a heavy-bottom 12-inch frying pan and sauté onions, mushrooms, and garlic over medium heat until they start to brown (don't let the garlic burn—it tends to become bitter). Towards the end of the browning process, sprinkle with the remaining 1/2 teaspoon paprika. Shake pan well and continue to brown for a minute or two until nicely golden. Stir in the beef broth, wine, tomato paste, Worcestershire sauce, and thyme.

Shake the 3 tablespoons flour in a small jar with 1/4 cup water until smooth. Stir into liquid in pan and simmer until it starts to thicken to a sauce-like consistency. Remove from heat and carefully stir in the browned beef.

Empty into a 9 × 13-inch baking dish. Cover tightly with foil and bake for 1 1/2 hours. Remove and chill until you are ready to proceed with pastry. This can be done an hour or two ahead, or early in the day.

Unroll the filo pastry carefully. Using one corner, count out 4 sheets. Keep sheets covered with a damp cloth. Lay 1 sheet of pastry down on work surface and lightly brush with oil, making sure to brush right to the edges. Sprinkle with 1 tablespoon of the bread crumbs. Lay a second sheet directly over the first and again brush lightly with oil and sprinkle with crumbs. Lay a third sheet on top of the second and continue with the brushing and sprinkling procedure. Place fourth layer on top of third and brush with oil but do not sprinkle with crumbs.

Preheat oven to 375°. Carefully fold all layers in half and lay this "package" on top of the cooled beef mixture (it fits a 9 × 13-inch pan very well). Brush top with a bit of additional oil or spray with non-stick cooking spray. Bake for 30 minutes.

Note: Return unused filo to refrigerator and use within two weeks.

Each serving provides:

386	Calories	25 g	Carbohydrate
35 g	Protein	368 mg	Sodium
15 g	Total fat	85 mg	Cholesterol

Savory Stew with Red Wine

This dish is so easy to assemble. The addition of red wine elevates this dish to the entertaining level. You can double or triple the ingredients to accommodate the number you plan to serve. Get a good French bread for sopping up that flavorful sauce.

Makes 5 to 6 servings

2	pounds of bottom round steak, trimmed of all visible fat and sinew and cut into 1-inch cubes
2	medium onions, sliced
2	large cloves garlic, minced
2	tablespoons chopped fresh parsley
1	teaspoon salt
1/2	teaspoon black pepper
1/2	teaspoon thyme
1	bay leaf, crumbled
1	teaspoon Kitchen Bouquet (see note)
1	can (10 ounces) sliced mushrooms, drained
1	can (14 ounces) tomato sauce
1	can (10 ounces) beef broth or homemade beef stock
3	tablespoons flour
1	cup dry red wine

Preheat oven to 325°. Combine all of the ingredients, except flour and red wine, in a large, heavy casserole. Shake flour and red wine together in a jar until smooth and stir into remaining ingredients. Cover tightly and bake for 3 hours, stirring occasionally.

Note: Kitchen Bouquet is a browning sauce for meat and gravy.

Each serving provides:			
312	Calories	15 g	Carbohydrate
37 g	Protein	1424 mg	Sodium
10 g	Total fat	92 mg	Cholesterol

Baked Shin Beef

This dish is easy to prepare and needs only mashed potatoes to complete this tasty meal. "This is better than steak," exclaimed one appreciative guest when served this dish.

When removing the fat from the beef, you might want to remove any soft marrow in the center of the bone, so you won't be tempted to eat it when cooked—it's 25 to 35 percent fat! It is also delicious (wouldn't you just know you shouldn't eat it?).

Makes 4 servings

Baked Beef

4	large slices of lean shin beef, center cut, bone in
3	large or 4 small carrots, peeled and sliced
3	onions, peeled and sliced
3	large or 4 small parsnips, peeled and sliced

Sauce

2	cans (10 ounces each) beef broth, undiluted
1/2	cup tomato sauce
1	tablespoon brown sugar
1	tablespoon lemon juice or malt vinegar
2	teaspoons dried basil

Preheat oven to 250°. Remove any visible fat from meat. Place beef slices in a large shallow baking pan in a single layer. Cover with carrots, onions, and parsnips.

Combine all of the sauce ingredients in a medium saucepan. Heat to just under the boiling point.

Pour the sauce over the beef and vegetables. Cover securely and bake for 4 to 6 hours.

Each serving provides:

285	Calories	31 g	Carbohydrate
29 g	Protein	820 mg	Sodium
5 g	Total fat	46 mg	Cholesterol

Leslie's Szechuan Beef

Makes 4 servings

Beef Strips
1   large top sirloin steak, partially frozen
1   egg, beaten
2   tablespoons flour
2   tablespoons cornstarch

Sauce
2   tablespoons cornstarch
1/4   cup lite soy sauce
1/4   cup sugar
1/2   cup red wine vinegar
1   to 2 teaspoons dry chilies (see note)
5   to 6 cloves garlic, minced
4   green onions, chopped

Preheat oven to 400°. Cut steak into thin strips at a slight angle (this is much easier to do when the meat is partially frozen). Combine egg, flour, and cornstarch. Add the strips and combine well.

Spray a cookie sheet with nonstick cooking spray. Arrange strips on the cookie sheet and lightly spray strips as well. Bake for 30 to 35 minutes or until strips are browned and crispy. Remove from pan and set aside in a warm place while you make the sauce.

Combine all of the sauce ingredients and microwave for 3 minutes, or cook on top of the stove, stirring until thickened. Pour over cooked strips and serve with rice.

Note: Start with 1 teaspoon of the dry chilies first, then add more to taste.

Each serving provides:

431	Calories	28 g	Carbohydrate
47 g	Protein	715 mg	Sodium
14 g	Total fat	182 mg	Cholesterol

Beer Steak

Serve this dish with mashed potatoes or noodles and green beans.

Makes 5 to 6 servings

Steak
2   pounds round steak, 1 inch thick
1   large onion, peeled and thinly sliced
1   bay leaf
1/4   teaspoon thyme
1   cup beer

Sauce
2   tablespoons butter or margarine
2   tablespoons flour
1   can (10 ounces) low-salt beef broth or consommé, undiluted
1   tablespoon tomato paste or 3 tablespoons ketchup

Preheat oven to 275°. Spray a nonstick skillet with nonstick cooking spray and brown steak quickly on both sides over high heat. Remove steak from pan and place in a shallow baking dish. Respray pan and cook onion over medium heat until it starts to wilt. Arrange onions on top of steak. Add bay leaf, thyme, and beer.

Make a sauce by melting butter in a small saucepan and then stirring in flour until well mixed. Stir in broth a little at a time to mix well, then stir in the tomato paste. Pour over the beef mixture, cover, and bake until tender, about 1 1/2 to 2 hours. Remove bay leaf before serving.

Note: If you have to open a can of tomato paste for 1 tablespoon, it is a good idea to lay a piece of plastic wrap on a cookie sheet and measure out the remaining can, 1 tablespoon at a time onto cookie sheet. Freeze, then wrap individually and store in a plastic bag in freezer. It is all premeasured for recipes using only 1 or 2 tablespoons.

Each serving provides:

281	Calories	7 g	Carbohydrate
36 g	Protein	163 mg	Sodium
10 g	Total fat	96 mg	Cholesterol

Beef, Tomato, and Onion Casserole

No browning of meat and no sautéing of vegetables is needed for this simple supper dish. Just serve with hot, fluffy rice.

Makes 3 servings

1	pound round steak, trimmed of all visible fat and sinew
2	tablespoons whole wheat flour
1/2	teaspoon black pepper
1	large onion, diced
1	can (14 ounces) stewed tomatoes
3	tablespoons lite soy sauce
1	teaspoon low-salt beef stock concentrate
1	tablespoon molasses

Preheat oven to 325°. Cut steak into thin strips at a slight angle (this is much easier to do when meat is partially frozen). Combine flour and pepper in a plastic bag. Add beef strips and shake well.

Empty into a casserole dish. Add onion and tomatoes. Combine soy sauce, beef stock, 1 cup hot water, and molasses and stir into beef-tomato mixture. Cover and bake for 2 to 2 1/2 hours or until beef is tender.

Each serving provides:

319	Calories	26 g	Carbohydrate
39 g	Protein	1066 mg	Sodium
7 g	Total fat	85 mg	Cholesterol

Short Ribs

This particular cut has a different texture than other cuts we have used. It tends to be on the firm side when cooked and "shreds" a bit. What you lose in texture, you make up for in flavor. Don't try to hurry this dish along by baking at a higher temperature; you must use a 250° oven.

The sauce is thin and perfect for making puddles in mashed potatoes (a must with this dish), and the onions are wonderful—like candy! Add some tender carrots for color and added nutrition.

Makes 4 to 6 servings

2	to 3 pounds short rib-style beef brisket point
	sprinkling of black pepper
3	to 4 large onions, peeled and sliced
2	tablespoons olive oil
1/2	cup lite soy sauce
2	tablespoons barbecue sauce
1	cup honey
1	or 2 large cloves garlic, minced

Preheat oven to 250°. Place beef in large casserole dish. Sprinkle lightly with black pepper. Cover beef with sliced onions. Combine oil, soy sauce, barbecue sauce, honey, and garlic and pour over beef and onions. Bake, covered, for 4 to 5 hours, or until beef is tender. Stir at the beginning of the last hour, so the onions are well-coated with the sauce.

Each serving provides:

571	Calories	50 g	Carbohydrate
49 g	Protein	948 mg	Sodium
19 g	Total fat	144 mg	Cholesterol

Rouladen with Mushroom Wine Sauce

Serve this dish with parsleyed potatoes, cut Romano beans, and a tossed salad or coleslaw.

Our friend Sheila Sterling sometimes substitutes a package of Knorr's Hunter Sauce for the mushroom wine sauce when making this dish for her family.

Makes 2 to 4 servings

Rouladen

1	teaspoon butter
1	cup chopped onion
$1/8$	teaspoon garlic powder
1	teaspoon Worcestershire sauce
1	cup whole wheat bread crumbs
$1/4$	teaspoon freshly ground black pepper
4	very thin slices top round rouladen

Mushroom Wine Sauce

1	tablespoon butter or margarine
$1/4$	pound mushrooms, sliced
2	teaspoons lemon juice
$1/2$	cup red wine
1	can ($7 1/2$ ounces) tomato sauce
2	tablespoons sugar

Preheat oven to 350°. Spray a nonstick skillet with nonstick cooking spray, then heat butter over medium heat and add onion. Sauté until onion is soft. Add garlic powder. Stir in Worcestershire sauce until onions are coated. Remove from heat and stir in bread crumbs and pepper. Let cool.

Lay the thin beef slices flat and distribute the onion–bread crumb mixture evenly over the tops. Roll up the meat, starting at the narrow end, and place seam side down in a shallow baking dish.

To make the sauce, melt butter in a small nonstick skillet. Sauté mushrooms for 1 minute, sprinkle with lemon juice, and continue to cook until liquid evaporates and mushrooms are golden. Stir in wine and let boil until wine is reduced by half its volume. Stir in tomato sauce and sugar. Bring to a simmer, then remove from heat.

Spoon sauce over beef rolls. Cover dish tightly with foil and bake for 1 hour.

	Each serving provides:		
288	Calories	21 g	Carbohydrate
29 g	Protein	554 mg	Sodium
9 g	Total fat	75 mg	Cholesterol

Hungarian Goulash

The introduction of non-fat sour cream has opened up a few dishes to the low-fat category that otherwise would not qualify, such as the following. Make sure you use Hungarian paprika.

Serve with poppy seed noodles, fresh green beans, and cucumber salad.

Makes 4 to 6 servings

2	tablespoons olive oil
3	cups very finely chopped onion
3	tablespoons Hungarian sweet paprika
1	can (14 ounces) tomato sauce plus $^1/_2$ can water
$^1/_2$	teaspoon salt
1	teaspoon black pepper
$^1/_2$	cup chopped sweet red pepper
$^1/_8$	teaspoon caraway seeds
2	pounds lean beef (hip of beef is a good cut), cut into $1^1/_2$-inch cubes
$^1/_2$	cup non-fat sour cream

Preheat oven to 250°. Heat the olive oil in a nonstick skillet and sauté the onions until nicely browned but not burned. Sprinkle with 1 tablespoon of the paprika during the final browning stages. Remove from heat and stir in the tomato sauce, water, salt, pepper, red pepper, and caraway seeds.

Empty beef cubes into a fairly deep casserole dish and stir in remaining 2 tablespoons paprika to coat meat. Stir in tomato sauce mixture. Cover tightly with foil, then place lid over the top. Bake for 3 to 4 hours (test after 3). Stir in sour cream just before serving.

Each serving provides:

343	Calories	16 g	Carbohydrate
37 g	Protein	667 mg	Sodium
15 g	Total fat	91 mg	Cholesterol

Swiss Steak

Like mother used to make (and for those who can't stand even a trace of pink in their steaks). This recipe serves four, but you'd better count on three, because somebody will want seconds—it's that kind of dish.

At the risk of seeming repetitious, the very best accompaniments to this dish are creamy whipped potatoes and green peas.

Makes 4 servings

1 1/2	pounds inside round steak
1/4	cup whole wheat flour
1 1/2	teaspoons dry mustard
1/4	teaspoon black pepper
1	medium onion, sliced
1/4	cup diced celery
1 1/2	teaspoons liquid Bovril or instant beef stock
1	teaspoon brown sugar
1	can (14 ounces) stewed tomatoes
1	teaspoon Worcestershire sauce

Preheat the broiler. Cut steak into serving sizes (about 4 pieces). Pound steaks well (you want to break down the fibers in this lean dense cut of meat). Combine flour, mustard, and pepper on a plate. Dip meat in the flour mixture, shaking off and saving any excess. Brown under the broiler on both sides, about 4 minutes per side. Reduce oven temperature to 325° to 350°.

Remove meat to a casserole dish. Spray a nonstick skillet with nonstick cooking spray. Add onions and celery and cook until onions are golden brown, stirring frequently. Stir in remainder of the unused flour mixture. Slowly stir in 1 cup water, Bovril, brown sugar, tomatoes, and Worcestershire sauce. Cook, stirring until thickened. Pour over steaks. Bake, covered, until tender, about 1 1/2 hours.

Each serving provides:

342	Calories	18 g	Carbohydrate
40 g	Protein	581 mg	Sodium
11 g	Total fat	102 mg	Cholesterol

Guinness Stew

Guinness stew from a Caithness! You just know it's good (thank you Shawn).

Makes 6 servings

2	medium to large onions, sliced
3	cloves garlic, minced
1/2	teaspoon pepper
1/2	teaspoon paprika
4	tablespoons plus 2 tablespoons flour
2 1/2	to 3 pounds lean stew meat, trimmed of all visible fat and sinew, cut into 1 1/2-inch cubes
1	bottle of Guinness stout (don't use canned)
1	tablespoon vinegar
1	tablespoon brown sugar
1 1/2	tablespoons fresh thyme or 1 teaspoon dried thyme
1	bay leaf
2	tablespoons chopped fresh parsley
1	can (10 ounces) beef broth, undiluted
2	thin slices day-old bread
1	to 2 tablespoons Dijon mustard or English mustard (see note)

Preheat oven to 300°. Spray a large nonstick skillet with nonstick cooking spray and sauté the onions over medium heat until limp. Add garlic and continue to sauté until onions are lightly browned. Remove to a casserole.

Place pepper, paprika, and 4 tablespoons of the flour in a plastic bag. Add beef cubes and shake to dust the meat lightly.

Spray pan again and brown beef on all sides over medium to high heat. Add to onions in casserole. Gradually stir Guinness into the pan. Stir in vinegar, brown sugar, thyme, bay leaf, and parsley. Place the 2 tablespoons flour in a small jar and add half of the beef broth; shake well, then stir into pan with the remaining beef broth. Bring to a boil, stirring, until slightly thickened.

Pour sauce over meat and onions. Cover tightly and bake for $2^1/_2$ to 3 hours or until meat is tender when pierced with a fork.

Spread bread slices with mustard and place over top of stew. Increase oven temperature to 450° and bake uncovered for an additional 15 to 20 minutes. Remove bay leaf before serving.

Note: If you decide on the English (dry mustard), mix it with just enough water to make a spreadable consistency (much like the consistency of Dijon), then spread on the bread.

Each serving provides:

388	Calories	23 g	Carbohydrate
45 g	Protein	610 mg	Sodium
10 g	Total fat	115 mg	Cholesterol

Stir-Frying

Stir-frying is much like sautéing, but it's done at a much higher heat, and the ingredients are kept almost constantly in motion to keep from overcooking. Toss would be a better word than stir. Food is literally lifted up from the hot surface of the wok and dropped back in with a tossing movement of the spatula. If food sticks, add a few drops of water or bouillon rather than additional oil.

A wok, which looks like a big metal salad bowl, uses less oil than a skillet and suits today's lifestyle. It is important to heat the wok before adding the oil; then heat the oil before adding food. If you fail to do this, the stir-fried vegetables will not be crisp and the whole dish will be far from perfect. Stir-frying is quick, it can be lowfat, and it is economical. It can be cleverly stretched to accommodate extra guests with the addition of extra vegetables and increasing the amount of rice or noodles. And with all of those good crisp vegetables, there is no need for salad! A wok is not a prerequisite, however, as stir-frying can be done successfully in a large nonstick skillet or electric frying pan. Remember to have everything assembled ahead of time, cook quickly, and serve immediately.

Knotty, gnarled knobs of ginger do not look very appetizing, but they are a very important ingredient in stir-frying. Powdered ginger can be used as a substitute, about 1/4 teaspoon per 1 tablespoon grated or finely minced, but it's best to save powdered ginger for your baking needs. Fresh ginger keeps well in a cool, dry place and should be peeled before using, although we always keep a piece frozen to avoid ever running out, and we sometimes grate without peeling.

Dried black mushrooms add an exotic flavor and aroma in stir-fried dishes. They keep very well in a dried state but must be soaked in hot water for 30 minutes before using.

Two methods of cooking vegetables are available; which one you use depends on the type of vegetable involved. Examples of quick-cooking vegetables are mushrooms, bean sprouts, snow peas, and green onions, which are stirred constantly over high heat. Vegetables such as broccoli, carrots, cauliflower, green beans, celery, and asparagus require longer cooking and should be steamed first. When thinly slicing vegetables, remember to always slice on the bias.

Following are some helpful hints for stir-frying.

- One cup of raw rice equals 3 cups cooked. White rice should be cooked in double the amount of liquid; brown rice should be cooked in triple the amount of liquid, and it takes twice as long to cook as the white rice. Wild rice takes $2^1/_4$ cups water to 1 cup rice and should be washed three times in warm water; it takes 45 minutes to cook.

- When selecting fresh mushrooms, choose ones with caps tightly closed at the bottom. Store them in a brown paper bag (paper sandwich bags are good for this purpose); do not store them in plastic bags. Never wash mushrooms—they absorb too much water. Wipe gently with a brush or peel if necessary.

Company Stir-Fry

It's good! It's easy! Serve with hot, fluffy rice and a tossed green salad.

Makes 4 servings

2	tenderloin steaks, about 8 ounces each
2	tablespoons olive oil
1	large onion, thinly sliced
2	small green peppers, seeded and thinly sliced
1	clove garlic, minced
1	pound fresh mushrooms, sliced (see note)
4	medium to large tomatoes, coarsely chopped
	salt and freshly ground black pepper, to taste

Slice the steaks thinly, at an angle (this is easier to do if they are partially frozen). Heat the oil in a large nonstick skillet and sauté the beef quickly over high heat. Don't spoil the tenderloin by overcooking it. Put the beef aside on a heated platter.

Stir-fry the onions, green peppers, and garlic over high heat. When these have been cooking about 2 minutes, add the mushrooms and cook an additional 2 minutes. Add the tomatoes, stirring constantly because they are going to produce a nice sauce. This will take only a minute or two. Return the meat and stir until nicely coated with this sauce. Add salt and pepper to taste.

Note: An egg slicer makes a good mushroom slicer!

Each serving provides:

318	Calories	19 g	Carbohydrate
28 g	Protein	75 mg	Sodium
16 g	Total fat	72 mg	Cholesterol

Beef and Pea Pod Stir-Fry

Like all stir-fries, this dish is best when it is made just prior to serving.

Flank steaks usually weigh about 2 pounds. Cut it in half and freeze until needed. Sirloin or tenderloin may be substituted for the flank. Remember to slice the beef thinly at an angle.

Makes 3 to 4 servings

1	pound flank steak
4	teaspoons dry mustard
2	teaspoons cornstarch
2	tablespoons soy sauce
3	tablespoons canola oil
1	clove garlic, peeled
6	green onions, trimmed and cut into 1-inch pieces (including some of the green)
1/4	pound fresh mushrooms, wiped (cut larger mushrooms in half)
1/4	pound snow pea pods, tips and strings removed (see note)

Four hours before you plan to cook, trim the steak of all fat and rub the meat on both sides with dry mustard.

Just prior to cooking, slice the steak into very thin slices, cutting across the grain and at an angle. If you place in the freezer for about 30 minutes, until partially frozen, the steak slices very easily.

Stir cornstarch into the soy sauce in a small bowl or custard cup and set aside.

Heat wok, then add oil and garlic. Stir garlic over high heat for 30 to 60 seconds to flavor the oil, but don't let it burn.

Remove garlic and add beef. Stir beef over high heat using two wooden spoons. The slices might stick together a bit from the mustard, but they will separate easily when pushed around with the spoons. Cook the meat, stirring most of the time, until all trace of pink disappears from the surface, about 3 minutes.

Add the vegetables and stir with the beef, still over very high heat. Cook for 3 to 4 minutes, stirring most of the time. These vegetables do not require much cooking and need to retain much of their texture, so don't overcook

Stir cornstarch and soy sauce until well blended and add to wok. Cook for 1 minute, stirring constantly, until cornstarch thickens and is well distributed among the meat and vegetables. Serve immediately over hot rice.

Note: If you use frozen peas, rinse in cold water just to thaw, then pat dry with paper towels.

Each serving provides:			
394	Calories	7 g	Carbohydrate
33 g	Protein	612 mg	Sodium
26 g	Total fat	77 mg	Cholesterol

Beef and Lettuce Wraps

*Our Sunday night testers loved this dish. Whether it was the novelty of
wrapping up the filling in the lettuce leaves taco-style or that the combination was so darned good, they just kept coming back for more.*

Makes 6 to 7 servings

2	tablespoons chutney
1	tablespoon brown sugar
1	tablespoon cornstarch
1	tablespoon hoisin sauce (see note)
1	tablespoon rice wine vinegar (see note)
1	tablespoon soy sauce
3/4	cup chicken bouillon
2	tablespoons olive oil
1	medium red onion, finely chopped
2	large cloves garlic, minced
1 1/2	to 1 3/4 pounds very lean ground beef
1/2	cup diced water chestnuts
1/2	cup blonde raisins
1/4	teaspoon crushed dried red pepper
1	cup fresh bean sprouts
1	large head iceberg lettuce

In a small bowl or measuring cup, combine chutney, brown sugar,
cornstarch, hoisin sauce, rice wine vinegar, soy sauce, and chicken
bouillon; set aside.

Heat oil in large skillet or wok over medium-low heat. Add onion
and garlic and stir-fry until onion starts to soften, about 2 minutes.
Increase heat to high and add ground beef. Stir-fry, breaking up meat
with a wooden spoon, until no trace of pink is left in the meat.

Stir in the water chestnuts, raisins, and crushed red pepper. Stir
in the bouillon mixture and keep stirring over high heat until sauce
thickens, about 3 minutes. If you are serving right away, stir in the
bean sprouts; if not, cool the beef mixture and store in the refrigerator.

An hour or two before you plan to serve, prepare the lettuce by
cutting out the core and rinsing lettuce, upside down, under cold running water, gently separating the leaves a little. Drain and store in a
large, paper-towel lined plastic bag in the refrigerator.

At serving time, reheat the beef mixture, then stir in the bean
sprouts until everything is well heated through. Place hot beef

mixture in a serving dish and place lettuce leaves in a large separate bowl. Each guest spoons some of the beef mixture onto a chilled lettuce leaf and rolls it up jelly roll-fashion and eats with fingers. Have additional hoisin sauce in a separate small dish and guests may brush lettuce leaves lightly with hoisin sauce before placing beef mixture on top.

Note: Hoisin sauce and rice wine vinegar may be found in the Asian food section of the supermarket.

	Each serving provides:		
279	Calories	21 g	Carbohydrate
15 g	Protein	383 mg	Sodium
15 g	Total fat	44 mg	Cholesterol

Beef Chow Mein

Makes 4 servings

1	pound lean ground beef
1	medium onion, diced
2	ribs of celery, diced
$^1/_2$	cup diced green pepper
1	cup shredded cabbage
1	cup fresh mushrooms, sliced
$^1/_2$	pound bean sprouts
1	can (14 ounces) water chestnuts, sliced
2	tablespoons lite soy sauce
1	tablespoon cornstarch
1	cup lite chicken broth
3	cups steam-fried noodles

In a wok or large non-stick skillet, brown ground beef over medium to high heat, breaking apart beef as it browns. Drain off any accumulated fat, if any. Add onions, celery, green pepper, and cabbage and stir-fry lightly until tender-crisp. Add mushrooms, bean sprouts, and water chestnuts and stir-fry to heat through.

Combine soy sauce, cornstarch, and chicken broth and add to pan. Stir into ground beef and vegetable mixture. Stir in noodles and cook for an additional 5 minutes.

Each serving provides:

547	Calories	60 g	Carbohydrate
37 g	Protein	880 mg	Sodium
18 g	Total fat	92 mg	Cholesterol

Beef and Tomato Stir-Fry

This meat must be marinated overnight (the addition of vinegar, lemon juice, or wine to a marinade tenderizes less tender cuts of beef). If you are looking for a beef and tomato stir-fry that can be prepared sooner, look at the Company Stir-Fry recipe on page 135.

Serve with hot, fluffy rice.

Makes 4 to 6 servings

1	pound flank steak or round steak
3	tablespoons lite soy sauce
1/4	cup white vinegar
1/4	cup brown sugar
2	tablespoons cornstarch
1	tablespoon canola oil or safflower oil
1	medium onion, peeled and cut into 4 wedges, then sliced thinly
1/2	medium green pepper, sliced thinly into strips
2	cups fresh mushrooms, cut in half or in quarters
2	medium tomatoes, cut into wedges

Cut steak across the grain into thin strips (1/4 inch to 1/8 inch thick). Cut strips into 2-inch to 3-inch lengths (household scissors are handy for this purpose).

Combine soy sauce, vinegar, and brown sugar and stir until sugar is dissolved. Pour over beef and mix lightly with fork to coat evenly. Cover and refrigerate overnight. Stir occasionally.

Carefully pour marinade into a small bowl and mix with cornstarch. When cornstarch has been absorbed, pour the mixture back over the beef.

Heat wok over high heat, then add oil and heat. Stir-fry onions, green peppers, and mushrooms for about 1 minute. Add beef and cornstarch mixture and cook for about 2 to 3 minutes, until sauce thickens. Stir in tomatoes just until heated through (not cooked).

Each serving provides:			
273	Calories	19 g	Carbohydrate
22 g	Protein	370 mg	Sodium
12 g	Total fat	52 mg	Cholesterol

Beef and Vegetable Stir-Fry

The sirloin steak needs to be cut very thinly, which is best accomplished by slicing when partially frozen. Because it is marinated, it needs very little cooking—less than a minute.

Makes 3 servings

2	tablespoons lite soy sauce
2	teaspoons sesame oil
2	tablespoons red wine vinegar
2	teaspoons brown sugar
1	clove garlic, minced
4	drops Louisiana or Durkee's hot sauce
1	pound sirloin steak, trimmed of all visible fat and sliced very thinly at an angle
2	tablespoons canola oil or safflower oil
1	cup diced zucchini or broccoli florets
1	cup diced celery
1	cup diced fresh mushrooms
1	teaspoon cornstarch

Combine soy sauce, sesame oil, red wine vinegar, brown sugar, garlic, and hot sauce. Pour over beef, toss well, and let sit for 1 hour.

Heat wok over high heat, then add oil and heat. Stir-fry the zucchini (or broccoli), celery, and mushrooms until tender-crisp. (Add mushrooms a minute or two after the celery and zucchini.) Don't overcook. Remove vegetables with a slotted spoon to a warm platter.

Drain the beef, reserving the marinade. Stir the cornstarch into the reserved marinade and set aside while you cook the beef.

Add drained beef to the wok or a large nonstick skillet and stir-fry over medium-high heat, stirring and flipping the pieces to separate them. It will take only a minute to cook the thinly sliced beef. Add the marinade-cornstarch mixture to the wok, along with the cooked vegetables. Turn the heat to high and let mixture boil to cook the cornstarch and thicken, stirring constantly. Again, this will take only a minute, once mixture starts to boil.

Serve at once with hot, fluffy rice.

Each serving provides:			
416	Calories	9 g	Carbohydrate
41 g	Protein	508 mg	Sodium
24 g	Total fat	115 mg	Cholesterol

Spicy Orange Beef and Broccoli

If you like to have ample sauce to spoon over your rice, this dish will not dis-
appoint—in any way.

Makes 4 servings

Beef and Broccoli
3/4   to 1 pound sirloin steak
2   tablespoons lite soy sauce
1/4   teaspoon sugar
2   teaspoons sesame oil
1   tablespoon grated fresh ginger
2   teaspoons cornstarch
1/2   teaspoon baking soda
1/4   teaspoon dried crushed red pepper
1¹/₂   tablespoons vegetable oil
4   to 5 cups broccoli florets
1   can (10 ounces) mandarin oranges, drained

Sauce
1/4   cup honey
1¹/₂   tablespoons lite soy sauce
2   tablespoons rice wine vinegar
3/4   cup beef broth (you can dissolve 3/4 teaspoon beef granules in
        3/4 cup hot water)
2   tablespoons cornstarch
1/4   teaspoon black pepper

Slice beef across the grain and at an angle into thin strips.

In a medium bowl, mix soy sauce, sugar, sesame oil, ginger, corn-starch, baking soda, and crushed red pepper. Add beef strips, mix well, and let sit for 30 minutes to 1 hour.

Meanwhile, mix sauce ingredients and set aside.

Heat wok over high heat, then add oil (or use a large nonstick skillet). Add beef and stir-fry for 1 to 2 minutes or until very lightly browned on all sides. Add broccoli and continue stirring for 2 to 3 minutes. Stir in sauce ingredients and orange segments and bring to a boil, stirring constantly. Boil 1 minute to thicken. Serve over cooked rice.

Each serving provides:

405	Calories	39 g	Carbohydrate
30 g	Protein	918 mg	Sodium
16 g	Total fat	76 mg	Cholesterol

Oriental Beef and Pea Pods

Aside from the beef and the pea pods, this recipe is totally different from our Beef and Pea Pod Stir-Fry recipe earlier.

Makes 4 servings

1/2	cup orange juice
1	tablespoon lite soy sauce
1	tablespoon cornstarch
3/4	teaspoon garlic powder
1/2	teaspoon ground ginger
1/4	teaspoon onion powder
1	pound flank steak
1/4	pound snow peas, tips and strings removed
1	small red pepper, seeded and thinly sliced

Combine orange juice, 1/2 cup water, soy sauce, cornstarch, garlic powder, ground ginger, and onion powder in a small bowl and set aside.

Slice steak into very thin slices, cutting across the grain and at an angle (if you place the meat in the freezer for about 30 minutes, until partially frozen, it slices very easily). Spray a large nonstick skillet with nonstick cooking spray. Stir-fry flank steak over high heat until all trace of pink disappears from surface. This will take 2 to 3 minutes. Stir in snow peas and red pepper and cook an additional 2 minutes. Stir in orange juice mixture and stir over high heat, stirring constantly until thickened. Serve over rice.

Each serving provides:

261	Calories	10 g	Carbohydrate
27 g	Protein	230 mg	Sodium
12 g	Total fat	66 mg	Cholesterol

Ground Beef

Ground beef, more commonly referred to in North America as hamburger meat, is a familiar ingredient in many favorite meals. Tasty casserole dishes, soups, spaghetti with meatballs or meat sauce, meat loaf, and that most popular sandwich of all time, a ground beef patty smothered in onions (either fried or raw) and smeared with ketchup and/or mustard. There has been a lot of controversy as to when and where the hamburger was born. The Germans supposedly brought it to the United States (from Hamburg), but the Italians claim that the hamburger patty was discovered when a spaghetti meatball fell on the floor and was accidentally stepped on!

Make sure you use extra-lean ground beef in dishes where you can't pour off any residual fat. When using medium or regular ground beef in recipes calling for cooked beef, you can successfully cook it in the microwave using a colander placed over a plate, thus allowing the fat to drip off. Microwave on high power until all trace of pink disappears, about 4 to 6 minutes. You can use this method for lean ground beef as well, but it is not necessary with extra lean. One friend, whose husband is on a very strict diet, rinses her cooked ground beef with boiling water (however, this washes away much of the flavor).

Natural oxidation will sometimes cause packaged ground beef to discolor slightly. You will find bright red meat on the outside and darker meat on the inside. Ground beef that has a dull gray or brown appearance has been sitting on the counter for too long or has been made with meat that was not too fresh to start with.

Ground beef seems to have withstood the test of time as well as any and all attempts of amateur and professional chefs to give it pizzazz. It can be stretched . . . and stretched . . . and stretched. Make sure, however, that you are not paying high prices for fat. Terms and definitions as to fat content seem to vary from market to market, so examine the meat yourself to gauge the amount of white fat embedded in the lean red meat. The lighter the color of ground meat, the more fat it contains. You may have your butcher grind it specially for you, or better yet, grind your own or chop your own with a pair of heavy chef's knives or two sharp knives the same length and weight. Make sure your knives are very sharp. You want to cut the meat cleanly, not mash it.

If you are looking for some new ground beef dishes to try, how about Hamburger Diane or Kathy's Fiery Fajitas? Maybe a lowfat chili or curry dish? Super-easy stuffed peppers? Whatever your tastes, we're sure you will find something to enjoy in this chapter.

Chinese Meatballs

The meatballs in all of these recipes are just a little different. The grated potato lightens the beef mixture and gives it a very nice texture. The dried onion flakes have the flavor of fried onions without the high fat content. You can mix and match your meatballs and sauces.

Makes 4 to 5 servings

Meatballs

1¹/₄	pounds lean ground beef
1	egg white
2	tablespoons soy sauce
1	small potato, peeled and grated (about ³/₄ cup)
1¹/₂	tablespoons dried onion flakes
¹/₄	teaspoon black pepper

Sauce

¹/₂	cup dark brown sugar
1	tablespoon dry mustard
1¹/₂	tablespoons cornstarch
³/₄	cup white vinegar

Preheat oven to 350°. Place the beef, egg white, soy sauce, potato, onion flakes, and pepper in a bowl and mix well. Form into 1-inch balls. Spray a nonstick frying pan with nonstick cooking spray and brown the meatballs over medium-high heat, turning to brown evenly. Give the pan a good shake to turn the balls nicely. Drain and discard any fat and place meatballs in a shallow baking dish.

To make the sauce, combine brown sugar, dry mustard, and cornstarch in a small saucepan. Gradually stir in vinegar and ³/₄ cup water. Bring to a boil, stirring constantly, and cook until slightly thickened, about 3 to 5 minutes.

Pour the sauce over the meatballs and bake for 30 to 40 minutes.

Each serving provides:			
436	Calories	33 g	Carbohydrate
22 g	Protein	512 mg	Sodium
24 g	Total fat	85 mg	Cholesterol

Sweet and Sour Meatballs #1

It is not necessary to crush the Rice Krispies. They just disappear when cooked—like magic. This is not only a very tasty dish but a very colorful one as well.

Makes 4 to 6 servings

Meatballs
1¹/2   pounds extra-lean ground beef
1   cup Rice Krispies
¹/3   teaspoon no-salt seasoning (page 260) or salt
¹/3   teaspoon black pepper
¹/3   teaspoon garlic powder
1   egg
¹/2   cup chicken stock
1   large green pepper, seeded and cut into squares
1   cup pineapple chunks, drained (save juice)

Sauce
3   tablespoons cornstarch
¹/2   cup sugar
¹/2   cup pineapple juice (saved from drained chunks)
¹/2   cup apple cider vinegar
3   tablespoons soy sauce
1   large or 2 small tomatoes, diced

In a medium bowl, combine beef, Rice Krispies, seasonings, and egg and mix well. Form into balls, roughly 1 inch in size. Spray a large nonstick skillet well with nonstick cooking spray and brown meatballs on all sides over medium heat. Give pan a quick shake to turn balls.

Add chicken stock, green pepper, and pineapple chunks. Cover skillet and as soon as mixture comes to a boil, reduce heat and simmer for 5 minutes.

To make the sauce, stir cornstarch and sugar together in a small saucepan. Gradually stir in the pineapple juice, vinegar, and soy sauce. Bring to a boil over medium heat, stirring constantly; as soon as it starts to thicken, pour over meatballs. Cover and as soon as sauce comes to a boil, reduce heat and simmer for 10 minutes.

Just before serving, stir in the tomatoes. You don't want to cook the tomatoes, just make sure they are well heated through. Serve over rice.

Each serving provides:

431	Calories	39 g	Carbohydrate
24 g	Protein	732 mg	Sodium
20 g	Total fat	114 mg	Cholesterol

Sweet and Sour Meatballs #2

These meatballs are quite different from the previous version. Perhaps you have your mind set on sweet and sour meatballs but don't have any canned pineapple, fresh green pepper, or fresh tomatoes—just try the version below. It's nice to have a choice, isn't it?

Makes 4 to 5 servings

Meatballs

1¼	pounds lean ground beef
1	egg white
6	tablespoons finely minced onion
¼	cup wheat germ or oatmeal
¼	cup 2 percent evaporated canned milk
1	tablespoon ketchup
½	teaspoon salt
¼	teaspoon black pepper

Sauce

1	can (10 ounces) tomato soup
½	cup (4 ounces) tomato sauce
2½	tablespoons lemon juice
6	tablespoons brown sugar

Mix the beef, egg white, onion, wheat germ, milk, ketchup, salt, and pepper together well and shape into 1-inch balls (you should have about 30 meatballs). Spray a nonstick frying pan with nonstick cooking spray and brown meatballs over medium-high heat, turning to brown evenly. Give the pan a good shake to turn the balls nicely. Drain and discard any fat from pan. Set aside.

To make the sauce, combine tomato soup, tomato sauce, lemon juice, and brown sugar in a saucepan large enough to accommodate the meatballs as well. Bring sauce ingredients to a boil, stirring constantly. Reduce to simmer; add meatballs and simmer, covered, for 30 to 40 minutes. Serve with rice and a green salad.

Each serving provides:

458	Calories	34 g	Carbohydrate
24 g	Protein	931 mg	Sodium
25 g	Total fat	87 mg	Cholesterol

Judy's Mom's Christmas Meatballs

Judy's mom doesn't serve these on Christmas Day (as the name might suggest) but at an annual Christmas party. It has become a tradition, and all of the guests search out the meatballs when they approach the buffet table. The meatballs have been modified slightly to suit today's lifestyles, but the sauce has remained the same for the last 25 years.

Serves 8 as a main course, 16 to 18 as an appetizer

Meatballs

2	pounds extra-lean ground beef
6	tablespoons chopped fresh parsley
2	eggs, lightly beaten
2	slices whole wheat bread, crumbled
1/2	cup natural bran
2	tablespoons soy sauce
1	large onion, finely minced (about 2 cups)
1/2	teaspoon black pepper
1/2	teaspoon garlic powder

Cranberry Sauce

1	can (14 ounces) whole-berry cranberry sauce
1	bottle (10 ounces) chili sauce
2	tablespoons dark brown sugar, firmly packed
1	tablespoon lemon juice

Preheat oven to 450°. Combine beef, parsley, eggs, bread, bran, soy sauce, onion, pepper, and garlic powder and mix well. Form mixture into small balls. Spray a broiler pan (or cookie sheet) with nonstick cooking spray. Place meatballs on pan or sheet and bake for 10 to 15 minutes. Drain and discard any fat and place meatballs in a casserole dish. Reduce oven temperature to 350°.

To make the sauce, heat the cranberry sauce, chili sauce, brown sugar, and lemon juice in a small saucepan. Pour sauce over the meatballs. Cover and bake for 15 minutes. (Or, you can make the sauce in a large saucepan, then add the meatballs to the sauce and heat over low heat for 15 minutes.)

Each main course serving provides:

454	Calories	46 g	Carbohydrate
29 g	Protein	900 mg	Sodium
18 g	Total fat	134 mg	Cholesterol

Curried Beef in a Pita

This dish can be an informal supper accompanied by a salad, or it can be a fun appetizer. Bring to a potluck supper or to one of the currently popular grazing parties (guests bring their favorite hors d'oeuvre, which are placed on a buffet table; while the problems of the world are being solved through lively conversation, people help themselves when the spirit moves them).

Makes 4 to 6 servings

Curried Beef
1	pound lean ground beef
1	clove garlic, minced
1	medium onion, finely chopped
$1/2$	teaspoon ground ginger
$1/2$	teaspoon curry powder
	salt, to taste
1	egg
1	cup non-fat plain yogurt or non-fat sour cream
6	individual pita bread pieces (see note)

Accompaniments
chopped apple
raisins
mango chutney (cut up any large pieces)

Brown ground beef in a nonstick skillet sprayed with nonstick cooking spray. Add garlic and onion and cook until onion is tender. Drain off any excess fat and discard. Add ground ginger, curry powder, and salt. Cover and cook over low heat for 10 minutes.

In a small bowl, beat the egg and blend in yogurt, stirring constantly. Add to meat mixture. Cook over low heat for 5 minutes, stirring constantly, but do not let boil.

Cut individual pitas in half. Let each person fill a pita with the ground beef curry and top with accompaniments of their choice.

Note: For appetizer servings, use a package of the mini pita breads.

Each serving provides:

333	Calories	27 g	Carbohydrate
26 g	Protein	312 mg	Sodium
13 g	Total fat	98 mg	Cholesterol

Bill's Black Bean Chili

*This should probably be called Molly MacMillan's Chili, because if her birth
had not been imminent, her mom may not have been craving chili, so her dad
(Bill) may not have created it.*

*When preparing the onions, you want quarter-moon slices rather than
circles, as this makes for a better texture in the chili. Serve with tossed green
salad and hot cornbread (we also like our chili topped with chopped, fresh,
mild onion). This dish freezes well.*

Makes 10 to 12 servings

2	pounds lean ground beef
4	medium onions, peeled, cut into quarters lengthwise, and then sliced
2	medium green peppers, seeded and cut into chunks
3	cans (14 ounces each) black beans, drained
2	packages (envelopes) chili mix
3	cans (10 ounces each) button mushrooms, drained
2	cans (10 ounces each) low-salt tomato soup
2	cans (14 ounces each) tomatoes
1/4	cup white vinegar
1	teaspoon chili powder
3	dried red chili peppers, crushed (see note)
1	teaspoon no-salt substitute (page 260) or salt
1/2	teaspoon pepper

Sauté ground beef over medium heat in a Dutch oven or large pot
until meat loses its pink color. Add onions and cook until onions turn
transparent in color. Drain off any accumulated fat. Add green peppers and continue to cook for 2 to 3 minutes. Add black beans, chili

mix, and mushrooms. Stir in tomato soup, tomatoes, vinegar, and
chili powder, and chili peppers. Stir in salt and pepper and as soon
as mixture comes to a boil, reduce heat and simmer for about 30 minutes, stirring occasionally.

Note: Crush the chili peppers between your fingers. Do not touch
your eyes until you have washed your fingers.

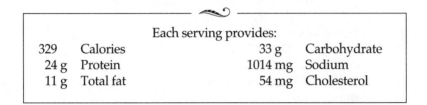

Each serving provides:

329	Calories	33 g	Carbohydrate
24 g	Protein	1014 mg	Sodium
11 g	Total fat	54 mg	Cholesterol

Meatballs in Creamy Sauce

This sinfully rich tasting sauce is neither sinful nor rich. Coffee is the secret flavor enhancer.

Makes 4 servings

Meatballs
1/2   cup 2 percent evaporated canned milk (see note)
1   teaspoon instant coffee granules
1 1/2 cups soft whole wheat bread crumbs
1 1/2 tablespoons olive oil
1/4   cup finely chopped onion
1   pound extra-lean ground beef
1/2   teaspoon paprika
1/4   teaspoon black pepper
1/8   teaspoon nutmeg
1/4   cup whole wheat flour

Sauce
1 1/2 teaspoons cornstarch
9   ounces 2 percent evaporated canned milk (see note)
2   bouillon cubes
1   teaspoon instant coffee granules

Preheat oven to 350°. Heat the milk in a small saucepan and dissolve coffee. Pour over bread crumbs. Heat the oil in a skillet over medium heat and sauté the onion until golden brown, then add to crumb mixture. Add beef, paprika, pepper, and nutmeg to crumb mixture. When mixed thoroughly, shape mixture into 1-inch balls and roll in the flour.

Line a cookie sheet with aluminum foil and lightly spray with non-stick cooking spray. Place meatballs on the sheet and bake for 20 minutes or until lightly browned. Empty the meatballs into a casserole dish.

To make the sauce, dissolve cornstarch in cold milk in a small saucepan. Add bouillon cubes and instant coffee. Bring to a boil. Immediately reduce heat and simmer, stirring constantly until sauce has thickened. Pour the sauce over the meatballs. Cover and bake for an additional 20 minutes.

Note: One can (13 ounces) of evaporated milk is sufficient for this recipe. Use 1/2 cup for the meatballs, then use the remainder for the sauce.

Each serving provides:

447	Calories		23 g	Carbohydrate
34 g	Protein		687 mg	Sodium
23 g	Total fat		97 mg	Cholesterol

Shepherd's Pie

*One couldn't write a beef cookbook without including a recipe for Shepherd's
Pie. Traditionally, it was served on Monday nights using Sunday's leftover
roast beef, which was ground up (a hand-held meat grinder, of course) and
mixed with onions fried in a goodly amount of butter. This was then moist-
ened with any remaining gravy. The mashed potatoes were spooned over the
top, and the whole dish was baked and served to an anxiously awaiting family. We have used fresh ground beef in this not so traditional but delicious
version. The spices (just right for this dish) all but eliminate the need for salt.
And the sweetness of parsnip is wonderful with beef (parsnips are especially
nice cooked and mashed with carrots as a vegetable to serve with roasts).*

Serve with green beans, carrots, and coleslaw.

Makes 4 servings

2	tablespoons canola oil or safflower oil
1	large onion, chopped
1	pound lean ground beef
1/2	teaspoon marjoram
1/2	teaspoon oregano
1/2	teaspoon thyme
1/8	teaspoon cayenne pepper
	pinch of salt
1	teaspoon Worcestershire sauce
1	medium to large parsnip, peeled and grated
1/2	cup consommé, undiluted
2	cups mashed potatoes
	Dash of paprika
	Sprinkling of parsley flakes

Preheat oven to 350°. In a large saucepan, heat the oil over
medium heat. Add the onion and sauté until soft and golden in
color, about 5 minutes. Add the ground beef and spices. Toss and
cook until beef loses all trace of pink. Stir in Worcestershire sauce
and parsnip. Cover and cook on low heat for about 10 minutes. Add
consommé and mix well.

Pour mixture into an 8 × 8-inch baking dish and spoon the mashed potatoes on top, spreading evenly with the back of a spoon (make sure the mashed potatoes are nice and creamy). Dust top of potatoes lightly with paprika and dried parsley flakes. Bake for 20 to 30 minutes, or until golden.

Each serving provides:

525	Calories	37 g	Carbohydrate
25 g	Protein	603 mg	Sodium
31 g	Total fat	87 mg	Cholesterol

Hamburger Diane

*Some people actually prefer a good ground beef patty to steak. Try giving
your hamburger a gourmet flare.*

*Serve with a tossed green salad. Or serve with baked potato and baby car-
rots instead of the French bread.*

Makes 4 servings

1	tablespoon Dijon mustard
2	teaspoons Worcestershire sauce
2	tablespoons chopped fresh parsley
1	pound extra-lean ground beef
	seasoned salt and seasoned pepper, to taste
2	teaspoons olive oil
1/2	cup chopped green onions
1/2	cup dry vermouth
1	loaf French bread
	pimento and parsley sprigs, optional

In a small dish or custard cup, mix the Dijon mustard, Worcestershire sauce, and parsley. Set aside.

Lightly mix beef, seasoned salt, and seasoned pepper in a large
bowl (too much handling tends to toughen the meat). Shape into 4
large patties, about 1 inch thick. Using a nonstick skillet, cook hamburgers over medium heat for 4 minutes on each side (you want
them medium to well done). Remove patties and keep warm in a
250° oven.

To make the sauce, remove fat from the bottom of the pan (blot
with paper towels). Add oil to pan and cook the green onions over

medium heat until soft. Add the vermouth and bring to a boil. Boil for 2 minutes, stirring occasionally. Stir in the mustard mixture. Return to boiling, while stirring constantly, until well heated through. Remove sauce from heat.

Place meat on thick French bread slices and spoon sauce over top. Garnish with pimento and parsley sprigs.

Each serving provides:			
509	Calories	39 g	Carbohydrate
31 g	Protein	604 mg	Sodium
21 g	Total fat	81 mg	Cholesterol

Helen's Hamburger Wrap-Ups

These freeze very well. Teenagers love them. This is perfect sports-watching food. The filling can also be spooned into tiny tart shells for tasty appetizers.

Makes 16 to 20 wrap-ups

1	pound of ground beef
1	cup chopped onions
1/2	teaspoon chili powder
1/4	teaspoon cayenne pepper
1	cup salsa (page 259)
2	loaves frozen bread dough, thawed

Preheat oven to 375°. Place ground beef in a colander sitting on a plate (to catch the fat) and cook in a microwave on high heat until all pink disappears (for more details, see the introduction at the beginning of this chapter). Put beef in a saucepan with onions, chili powder, cayenne pepper, and salsa and cook over medium heat until onions are soft. Place in a colander to drain.

Flatten a piece of bread dough (bun size) and place a large spoon-ful of the meat mixture in the center. Seal well and place on a cookie sheet which has been lightly sprayed with nonstick cooking spray. Let rise for 20 minutes. Bake for 20 minutes.

Each serving provides:

161	Calories	22 g	Carbohydrate
8 g	Protein	208 mg	Sodium
5 g	Total fat	16 mg	Cholesterol

Chili Con Carne

If your chili powder has been sitting on the shelf for a long time, it may not have its original pep. Curry powders are another spice that vary with age and also from brand to brand. Good cooks always taste and adjust seasonings before they are totally satisfied.

This dish freezes well.

Makes 6 to 8 servings

2	pounds extra-lean ground beef
1	cup chopped onion
1/4	cup chopped green pepper
2	apples, cored and sliced
1/2	teaspoon salt
3	cups tomato juice
1/2	cup chopped celery
2	tablespoons chili powder
2	cans (14 ounces each) kidney beans and its liquid

Brown the meat in a Dutch oven over medium heat. Drain off any fat and discard. Add onions, green peppers, apples, salt, tomato juice, celery, and chili powder and simmer gently for 1 hour. Add the kidney beans and simmer for an additional hour or until it reaches desired thickness.

Each serving provides:

390	Calories	29 g	Carbohydrate
32 g	Protein	949 mg	Sodium
17 g	Total fat	81 mg	Cholesterol

Burritos

Burritos are made by wrapping a filling such as a spicy meat mixture or re-
fried beans in a soft flour tortilla. Refried beans are now available fat free;
look for them in your supermarket.

When you are rolling burritos, fold sides of tortilla over filling to center,
then fold bottom over filling and roll up, enclosing filling completely. They
can be eaten in your fingers or placed on a plate and topped with a sauce.

Makes 8 to 10 servings

Burritos

1¹/₂	pounds extra-lean ground beef
¹/₂	teaspoon paprika
¹/₂	teaspoon black pepper
¹/₂	teaspoon garlic powder
1	teaspoon cumin
1	teaspoon chili powder
3	tablespoons onion flakes
1	can (4 ounces) green chilies, drained, seeded, and diced
1	can (14 ounces) stewed tomatoes
1	can (5¹/₂ ounces) tomato paste plus 1 can water
1	can (14 ounces) refried beans
16	flour tortillas
	shredded lettuce, optional

Non-Fat Sour Cream Sauce

1	cup non-fat sour cream
¹/₄	teaspoon lemon juice
¹/₂	teaspoon garlic powder
¹/₄	teaspoon oregano

Brown ground beef over medium-high heat in a Dutch oven with
the paprika and black pepper, breaking up the meat with a fork or
wooden spoon until no trace of pink remains. Drain off all fat.

Add garlic powder, cumin, chili powder, dehydrated onions,
chilies, tomatoes, and tomato paste and water and cook over
medium-high heat, uncovered, until most of the moisture has been
cooked away. Stir in refried beans. This can be made ahead and reheated later.

To make the sour cream sauce, stir the sour cream, lemon juice,
garlic powder, and oregano well together.

Warm tortillas by wrapping the stack in foil and placing in a 350° oven for 12 to 15 minutes, or just until heated through (not crisp). They can also be wrapped in a damp tea towel and placed in the oven (same time and temperature).

Arrange heated tortillas in a towel-lined basket alongside meat. Place the sour cream sauce and our delicious fresh tomato salsa in individual bowls to accompany burritos (see page 259). Shredded lettuce may be placed on top of filling before rolling the burritos.

Each serving provides:

397	Calories	46 g	Carbohydrate
24 g	Protein	602 mg	Sodium
13 g	Total fat	52 mg	Cholesterol

Kathy's Fiery Fajitas

This makes great sports-watching food. The filling can be made the day before and refrigerated (or weeks before and frozen) until needed. See our variations below for tacos and taco salad. (The taco salad calls for avocados, which are high in fat content but are nutritious — you can either omit or eat sparingly.)

Makes 6 servings

Fajitas

1	pound extra-lean ground beef
1	medium onion, peeled and chopped
2	tablespoons lime juice
1	tablespoon chopped cilantro or parsley
2	to 3 teaspoons chili powder
1	teaspoon ground cumin
1/4	teaspoon pepper
1/4	teaspoon salt, optional
1	bottle (12 ounces) salsa
1	can (12 ounces) "Mexicorn" corn niblets, drained
12	flour tortillas, 8 inches each

Garnishes

shredded lettuce
diced tomatoes
lowfat cheddar cheese, grated
non-fat sour cream

In a large nonstick skillet, cook ground beef and onions over medium-high heat until beef is browned and onion is tender. Drain off any accumulated fat. Add lime juice, cilantro, chili powder, cumin, pepper, salt, salsa, and corn and stir until heated through.

Heat tortillas according to package directions, or wrap in a damp tea towel and place in a 350° oven for 15 to 20 minutes, or until heated through (the latter method prevents tortillas from drying out).

Fill warm tortillas with meat mixture and serve with garnishes on the side.

Variations

Tacos: Substitute 1 package taco shells for tortillas. Prepare fajita ingredients as directed, but omit the corn niblets. Heat taco shells in a preheated 250° oven for 5 to 7 minutes. When ingredients are cooked, fill each taco shell with about 2 tablespoons of the beef filling. Top beef with same garnishes as for fajitas. Makes 4 to 6 servings.

Taco Salad: Follow directions for the taco filling. For each salad, top lightly crushed tortilla chips with shredded lettuce, meat mixture, and lowfat grated cheese. Garnish with avocado slices and chopped tomatoes around the edge of the salad. Serve immediately. Makes 4 servings.

Each serving provides:

516	Calories	69 g	Carbohydrate
26 g	Protein	696 mg	Sodium
16 g	Total fat	54 mg	Cholesterol

Beet Green Rolls

The fresh beet leaves and the fresh dill from the garden combine to make this dish a special treat. If you have your own vegetable garden, you will know the beet leaves and the dill are ready at the same time. Now that we have no-fat sour cream available, you might want to put a dollop on top. This is one of the eagerly awaited early summer treats from the garden. See the variation below for cabbage rolls.

Makes 8 servings

Meat Rolls

30	(more or less) young beet leaves
1¹/₂	pounds extra-lean ground beef
¹/₄	cup uncooked long-grain rice
4	tablespoons grated onion
2	tablespoons chopped fresh dill
¹/₂	teaspoon thyme

Sauce

1	can (5¹/₂ ounces) tomato paste
3	medium-size tomatoes, cut up
2	tablespoons chopped fresh dill
1	tablespoon sugar
1¹/₂	teaspoons no-salt seasoning (page 260) or salt, or a mixture of both
¹/₄	teaspoon pepper
¹/₄	teaspoon garlic powder
¹/₄	cup white wine or chicken broth

Bring 1 inch of water to a boil. Soften beet leaves in boiling water for 30 to 60 seconds or steam until wilted. Lay out on paper towels to absorb extra moisture.

Preheat oven to 325°. Combine ground beef, rice, onion, dill, thyme, and ¹/₄ cup water to form the filling.

Place a teaspoon of the meat-rice mixture on each leaf and roll up. Place in a casserole, seam side down. Place rolls close together.

To make the sauce, combine tomato paste, 3 cups water, tomatoes, dill, sugar, salt, pepper, garlic powder, and white wine or broth in a medium saucepan. Simmer, uncovered, for about 30 minutes. Pour sauce over rolls and bake, covered, for 1 hour.

Variation

Cabbage Rolls: Cabbage leaves may be substituted for the beet green leaves. Cut around core of large cabbage, then immerse in boiling water and parboil for 3 or 4 minutes. Let stand for 15 minutes. Peel off wilted leaves of cabbage and cut the ribs out of the large leaves before rolling. Fill with the meat-rice mixture and place in pan, seam side down. Place rolls close together and pour sauce over top. These will take 30 minutes longer to bake than the beet green leaves.

Each serving provides:			
261	Calories	13 g	Carbohydrate
18 g	Protein	249 mg	Sodium
15 g	Total fat	59 mg	Cholesterol

Beef and Mushroom Stuffed Peppers

Easy and tasty would best describe this dish. Buy crisp, shiny peppers—tired old peppers going into the oven are going to be tired old peppers coming out. You want a little snap to this vegetable. These will freeze, but not well (the peppers will lose their texture).

Serve with cooked rice and a sliced tomato salad.

Makes 4 servings

4	large green bell peppers, seeded and sliced in half lengthwise
1	pound lean ground beef
1	teaspoon paprika
1/2	teaspoon garlic salt
1 1/2	cups diced fresh mushrooms (see note)
1/4	cup chopped fresh parsley
1	teaspoon oregano
1	teaspoon chili powder
1 1/2	cups "thick and chunky" salsa

Preheat oven to 350°. Place the peppers in a 9 × 13-inch baking pan. If necessary, mold crumbled foil around bottoms to keep them upright.

Place beef in a large skillet, sprinkle with paprika and garlic salt and cook over medium-high heat until no trace of pink remains. Drain well in a colander or sieve. Wipe skillet with a paper towel, then return meat and stir in mushrooms, parsley, oregano, chili powder, and salsa. Cook over medium heat until warm. If the beef seems too dry, add 1 or 2 more tablespoons of the salsa. Divide filling evenly among the 8 pepper halves, packing down lightly with a spoon.

Cover baking pan tightly with foil or a lid and bake for 40 minutes, or until the peppers are soft. Don't overcook—you want the peppers tender-crisp.

Note: Never wash mushrooms—they absorb too much water. Wipe gently with a brush or peel if necessary.

Each serving provides:			
311	Calories	18 g	Carbohydrate
27 g	Protein	807 mg	Sodium
16 g	Total fat	81 mg	Cholesterol

Hurry Curry for Two

Kitchen Bouquet gives a rich brown color and combines nicely with the other ingredients to produce a delicious flavor.
   Serve with steamed rice and a tossed salad.

Makes 2 servings

1/2	pound extra-lean ground beef
1/2	cup chopped onion
1/4	cup finely minced celery
2	teaspoons curry powder
1	teaspoon Kitchen Bouquet (a gravy enhancer)
1	can (10 ounces) consommé, undiluted
1/2	cup chopped apple
1	tablespoon flour
1/4	cup sherry
5	prunes, slivered, or 2 tablespoons raisins

   Spray a small nonstick skillet with nonstick cooking spray and brown meat and onions over medium-high heat until onions are light brown. Drain off any fat. Add celery to the skillet.
   Combine curry powder, Kitchen Bouquet, and consommé and add to skillet. Let come to a boil. Add apples, reduce heat, and simmer for 15 to 20 minutes.
   Shake flour and sherry in a small jar until well combined and stir into curry mixture along with the prunes and simmer, stirring constantly, until mixture is thickened.

Each serving provides:

426	Calories	30 g	Carbohydrate
33 g	Protein	954 mg	Sodium
17 g	Total fat	81 mg	Cholesterol

Ground Beef Curry

Hot and spicy! If your taste runs to milder curries, reduce the cayenne to $1/8$ or $1/16$ of the amount in this recipe. If you like a curry to blow the top of your head off, increase the cayenne to almost $1/2$ teaspoon. If you ever get carried away and make your dish too spicy, you can cool it down a bit by topping it with a spoonful or two of plain yogurt. Don't drink water to cool your mouth—drink a bit of milk or take a spoonful of yogurt.

Serve with hot, fluffy rice (Basmati rice is excellent with curries) and condiments of your choice, for example, chutney, chopped fresh tomatoes, diced bananas, chopped cooked egg white, and chopped dry-roasted peanuts to name a few. Doreen's Special Salad (page 251) goes very well with a curry dinner.

Makes 4 servings

1	teaspoon olive oil
1	onion, peeled and chopped
1	teaspoon grated fresh ginger (see note)
1	pound lean ground beef
$1/4$	teaspoon cayenne pepper
$1/4$	teaspoon black pepper
2	tablespoons curry powder
1	teaspoon cumin
1	teaspoon ground coriander
2	cups beef stock
3	tablespoons tomato paste
$1/3$	cup raisins

Spray a large nonstick skillet with nonstick cooking spray and add the olive oil. Cook onion and ginger over medium heat, stirring occasionally, for 5 minutes. Add ground beef and cook, breaking up with a spoon (a two-tined pasta fork also works well), until browned, about 7 minutes. Drain off any fat.

Sprinkle meat mixture with cayenne, black pepper, curry powder, cumin, and coriander. Stir over medium heat until spices are well absorbed. Stir in beef stock and tomato paste and simmer, uncovered, for 20 minutes, stirring occasionally. Stir in raisins and continue to simmer for an additional 5 minutes. If it is not the consistency you want, continue to simmer until reduced further.

Note: It is handy to have some ginger in the freezer. When pressed for time, you can grate it, skin and all.

Each serving provides:

332	Calories	19 g	Carbohydrate
26 g	Protein	184 mg	Sodium
17 g	Total fat	84 mg	Cholesterol

Old-Fashioned Meat Loaf

Here's an old-fashioned dish offered in a new-fashioned recipe. Removing the fat from beef, unfortunately, removes the flavor and moisture as well. How to replace flavor and moisture? Grated mushrooms to the rescue! Serve with the easy mushroom sauce (below), baked potatoes, baked acorn squash, and peas.

Makes 4 to 5 servings

Meat Loaf

1	pound extra-lean ground beef
1	medium onion, finely chopped
1	slice whole wheat bread, crumbled
1/4	cup wheat germ
1/4	teaspoon thyme
1/2	teaspoon salt
1/4	teaspoon freshly ground black pepper
1	egg, lightly beaten
1	cup grated raw mushrooms, lightly packed (firm, fresh mushrooms grate very easily)
3	tablespoons chopped fresh parsley
1/2	cup skim milk
	dash of Worcestershire sauce

Easy Mushroom Sauce

1	can (10 ounces) reduced-fat cream of mushroom soup
1/2	teaspoon Worcestershire sauce
2/3	cup 2 percent evaporated canned milk
1	can (4 ounces) mushroom pieces, drained, or 1/4 cup sliced fresh mushrooms, lightly sautéed

Preheat oven to 350°. Combine ground beef, onion, bread, wheat germ, thyme, salt, pepper, egg, mushrooms, parsley, milk, and Worcestershire sauce and shape into a loaf, about 7 inches in length and 5 inches in width.

Place ground beef mixture in a baking dish (not a loaf pan) and bake for 45 minutes or until brown and firm to the touch. Remove from oven and pour off any fat (if you use good quality, extra-lean beef, there should be little, if any fat).

To make mushroom sauce, mix soup and Worcestershire sauce in a small saucepan. Gradually stir in milk, then mushroom pieces. Heat, but do not boil. Serve on the side with sliced meat loaf.

	Each serving provides:		
407	Calories	35 g	Carbohydrate
30 g	Protein	657 mg	Sodium
16 g	Total fat	115 mg	Cholesterol

Sweet Tomato-Glazed or
Chutney-Glazed Meat Loaf

Again, we have added grated vegetable to replace the moisture lost by using extra-lean ground beef. This recipe also gives you a choice between adding a sweet tomato glaze or a chutney glaze to the meat loaf.

Serve with cooked rice, French-style green beans, and a tossed green salad. If you have prepared the chutney glaze, broiled peaches (page 233) are a nice addition.

Makes 4 to 5 servings

Sweet Tomato Glaze
1/4   cup low-salt ketchup
1   teaspoon dry mustard
1/2   cup brown sugar

Chutney Glaze
3/4   cup chutney (cut up any large pieces)
3   tablespoons orange juice

Meat Loaf
1   pound extra-lean ground beef
1/2   cup shredded carrot
2   tablespoons grated celery
1   medium onion, very finely chopped
1   slice whole wheat bread, crumbled
1/4   cup bran
2   tablespoons chopped fresh parsley
1   egg, lightly beaten
1/2   cup tomato juice or V-8 juice
1   clove garlic, minced
1   teaspoon curry powder
1/2   teaspoon salt
1/3   teaspoon black pepper

To make the sweet tomato glaze, combine ketchup, 1/4 cup water, dry mustard, and brown sugar in a small bowl. Stir to dissolve sugar.

To make the chutney glaze, combine chutney and orange juice in a saucepan. Heat and stir mixture over medium heat until it is well heated through.

To make the meat loaf, preheat the oven to 350°. Combine the ground beef, carrots, celery, onions, bread, bran, parsley, egg, tomato juice, garlic, curry powder, salt, and pepper. Pack the mixture into a 9 × 5-inch loaf pan.

If you're using the sweet tomato glaze: bake the meat loaf for 45 minutes. Remove from oven, carefully pour off any fat. Spoon the sweet tomato glaze over the top of the meat loaf and return it to the oven for 15 to 20 minutes or until firm to the touch.

If you're using the chutney glaze: bake the meat loaf for 1 hour or until brown and firm to the touch. Pour off any excess liquid and invert onto a serving plate. Spoon half of the chutney glaze over the meat loaf and serve the remaining glaze at the table.

Each serving provides:

354	Calories	34 g	Carbohydrate
23 g	Protein	418 mg	Sodium
14 g	Total fat	107 mg	Cholesterol

Marlene's Low-Cal Zucchini and Beef

Makes 6 servings

2	pounds extra-lean ground beef
1	teaspoon seasoned salt
1	teaspoon onion powder
1/2	teaspoon paprika
1/8	teaspoon oregano
1/8	teaspoon pepper
1	envelope OXO beef bouillon mix
1 1/2	cups V-8 juice
7	cups very thinly sliced zucchini (about 1 3/4 pounds)
3	tomatoes, cut into small pieces

In a large frying pan, brown ground beef with all the dry seasonings over medium heat. Add V-8 juice and simmer for 5 minutes. Add zucchini and tomato and stir to mix in. Cover and cook over medium heat, stirring occasionally, for 20 to 30 minutes, or until zucchini is cooked.

Note: Excess juices can be thickened to a gravy-like consistency by dissolving 2 tablespoons cornstarch in 1/4 cup water and stirring into zucchini-beef mixture. Bring to a boil and let cook until thickened.

Each serving provides:

403	Calories	11 g	Carbohydrate
31 g	Protein	621 mg	Sodium
26 g	Total fat	105 mg	Cholesterol

Chinese Casserole

Here is an easy, tasty dish requiring only a minimal amount of preparation. This is the meal to prepare when you are in the mood for a little crunch and a lot of flavor.

Serve with chow mein noodles on top and soy sauce on the side.

Makes 4 servings

1/2	cup beef bouillon
1/2	cup instant rice
1	pound extra-lean ground beef
1	small onion, chopped
1/2	cup slivered almonds
1/2	cup Chinese plum sauce (see note)
1	cup bean sprouts
1	can (10 ounces) button mushrooms, drained
1	cup chopped celery

Preheat oven to 325°. Bring beef bouillon to a boil in a small saucepan. Stir in rice; cover and remove from heat. Let stand 5 minutes.

Brown beef and onion. Drain any excess fat (there should be very little, if any). Spray a casserole with nonstick cooking spray. Place beef mixture in the casserole and stir in rice. Gently stir in almonds, plum sauce, bean sprouts, mushrooms, and celery. Bake for 30 minutes.

Note: Chinese plum sauce is available in most supermarkets and all Asian specialty stores.

Each serving provides:

460	Calories	31 g	Carbohydrate
31 g	Protein	471 mg	Sodium
24 g	Total fat	81 mg	Cholesterol

Tourtière

A beef cookbook wouldn't be complete if it didn't contain this Christmas-time favorite. This meat pie is traditionally served in a regular two-crust pie, but filo pastry has far less fat content. It is usually served with a tomato butter or tomato chutney (see page 263). One year we teamed it up with a pear salad and it was a big success.

This dish may be frozen before or after baking—it freezes well both ways.

Makes 4 servings

1	pound extra-lean ground beef
3/4	cup beef broth
1	medium onion, finely chopped
1	cup grated mushrooms
1/4	cup oatmeal
2	cloves garlic, minced
1/4	teaspoon thyme
1/4	teaspoon oregano
1/8	to 1/4 teaspoon allspice
1/8	to 1/4 teaspoon cloves
3/4	teaspoon no-salt seasoning (page 260) or salt, or a mixture of both
5	sheets filo pastry
2	to 3 tablespoons dry bread crumbs
	dash of garlic salt
	dash of pepper

Preheat oven to 350°. Combine the raw ground beef, broth, onions, mushrooms, oatmeal, garlic, and spices in a medium, heavy-bottom saucepan. Cover and simmer very slowly for about 45 minutes. Stir frequently so it doesn't stick on the bottom. Let cool before adding to pie shell.

Keep filo pastry covered with a lightly dampened cloth to prevent it from drying out. Spray one sheet of filo lightly with nonstick cooking spray, sprinkle lightly with bread crumbs and top with a second sheet of pastry. Spray second sheet and sprinkle with crumbs. Top with a third sheet and spray but omit the crumbs. Gently mold into a 9-inch pie plate, letting edges hang over. Pour filling into pastry-lined pie plate. Spray the two remaining sheets of filo. Fold them in half, trim to fit top, place on top of filling, and bring the overhang up over top crust; spray with more nonstick cooking spray. Sprinkle lightly with the garlic salt and pepper.

Bake pie for 35 to 45 minutes, or until pastry is golden brown.

Each serving provides:			
398	Calories	24 g	Carbohydrate
26 g	Protein	371 mg	Sodium
21 g	Total fat	78 mg	Cholesterol

Applesauce Mini Meat Loaves

Applesauce adds a special flavor and moistening magic to these meat loaves (or large meatballs). Combine this with just the right amount of tang from the ketchup, and you come up with a winner. This recipe is sure to become a household classic ("Can't think what to have for dinner—guess I'll make that old standby, mini meat loaves.").

Serve with baked potatoes, baked squash, peas, and coleslaw.

Makes 4 servings

1	pound extra-lean ground beef
$2/3$	cup applesauce (fairly thick)
$1/2$	cup whole wheat soft bread crumbs
$1/2$	teaspoon salt
1	egg
$1/4$	cup minced onion
	freshly ground black pepper, to taste
	flour for dusting
$1/2$	cup ketchup

Preheat oven to 375°. Combine the ground beef, applesauce, bread crumbs, salt, egg, minced onion, and pepper well, then form into fairly large oval balls (about the size of an extra-large egg). Dust meatballs with flour. Spray a nonstick skillet well with nonstick cooking spray and brown meatballs on all sides over medium heat.

Place in a shallow 11 × 7-inch baking dish. Combine ketchup and $1/2$ cup water and pour over balls. Cover and bake for about 45 minutes.

Each serving provides:

330	Calories	16 g	Carbohydrate
27 g	Protein	731 mg	Sodium
17 g	Total fat	134 mg	Cholesterol

Spanish Hash with Lowfat Tortilla Chips

Serve this dish over hot, fluffy rice. A few pine nuts or toasted slivered almonds sprinkled lightly over the top will dress up this dish if you are planning for a party. The recipe also doubles or triples well.

Makes 4 servings

1	pound lean ground beef
1	cup finely chopped onion
1	medium to large green pepper, seeded and chopped
1	can (14 ounces) stewed tomatoes, broken into pieces with a fork
1/3	cup raisins
1 1/2	teaspoons chili powder
1/2	teaspoon cinnamon
1/4	teaspoon allspice
1	clove garlic, minced
1/8	teaspoon pepper
1/3	cup taco sauce
1	package corn tortillas, 6-inch rounds

Preheat oven to 350°. Sauté ground beef, onion, and green pepper in a large nonstick skillet, until no trace of pink remains in the beef. Drain in colander. Return to pan and add tomatoes, raisins, chili powder, cinnamon, allspice, garlic, and pepper and cook over medium heat, covered, for about 15 minutes, stirring occasionally. Stir in taco sauce and remove from heat when well-heated.

Cut tortillas into quarters or into six wedges (you can cut faster if you stack the tortillas). Spray a cookie sheet with nonstick cooking spray and spread tortilla pieces on top in a single layer. Spray lightly with the cooking spray and bake until golden brown and crisp. This will take 5 to 10 minutes (start checking after 5 minutes, as they brown quickly). Serve hash and chips together in separate bowls.

Each serving provides:			
533	Calories	64 g	Carbohydrate
31 g	Protein	616 mg	Sodium
17 g	Total fat	81 mg	Cholesterol

Beef-Berry Pizza

Keep this recipe in mind for the festive season.

Makes 4 servings

Caramelized Onions

2   tablespoons olive oil
3   medium onions, finely sliced
3¹/₂   tablespoons brown sugar
2   tablespoons rice wine vinegar (found in Asian food
       section of supermarkets)

Pizza

¹/₄   to ¹/₃ pound extra-lean ground beef
¹/₄   teaspoon no-salt seasoning (page 260)
¹/₄   teaspoon black pepper
¹/₄   teaspoon dried basil
1   round (12 inches) pizza dough
2   cups shredded lowfat mozzarella cheese
¹/₂   cup black olives, cut into circles
¹/₂   cup dried cranberries

Warm the olive oil in a small, heavy-bottom saucepan over low heat. Add the onions and stir well until onions are coated with oil. Stir in the brown sugar and increase the heat to high. Bring mixture to a boil and immediately reduce heat to simmer. Cook, tightly covered, stirring occasionally for 1¹/₂ hours. Stir in the rice wine vinegar until it is well absorbed. Continue to simmer, uncovered this time, for an additional 30 minutes. The mixture will have a marmalade-like appearance. This may be made ahead and refrigerated until needed.

To make the pizza, preheat oven to 450°. In a nonstick skillet cook ground beef, sprinkling with no-salt seasoning, pepper, and basil. Drain in a colander (or cook the ground beef and seasonings in a colander in the microwave, using a plate to catch drippings).

Place pizza dough on a baking sheet which has been sprayed with nonstick cooking spray. Spread onion marmalade evenly on dough, leaving a 1/2-inch border around the edge. Spoon ground beef over onion, sprinkle mozzarella cheese over beef, then top with olives and cranberries.

Bake in the lower third of the oven for 15 minutes.

	Each serving provides:		
633	Calories	75 g	Carbohydrate
28 g	Protein	786 mg	Sodium
24 g	Total fat	52 mg	Cholesterol

Veal

Veal is the meat from young calves. The choicest veal is the milk-fed (provimi). Grain-fed veal is a little darker in color. Calves, because of their age, have underdeveloped muscles and store no fat. However, the stored fat in beef keeps the meat moist during cooking, so all veal cuts except the scallops, chops, and cutlets are often larded before roasting to ensure tenderness. Veal was once available only in the spring, but now it is available year-round, although it's more plentiful in late winter to spring. When selecting, look for light grayish-pink lean tissue.

The cutlets and the scallops (known as escalope in France, scaloppine in Italy, and schnitzel in Germany) are the most popular cuts and are the most readily available. They must be pounded between sheets of waxed paper or plastic wrap before cooking. If you don't have a meat mallet, the bottom of a cast-iron fry-pan works well, as does an empty wine bottle. Veal does not wait well, so serve it as soon as it is cooked.

Veal Chops

Makes 2 servings

1   tablespoon soy sauce
2   teaspoons sesame oil
1   clove garlic, minced
1   teaspoon minced fresh ginger
1   green onion, chopped
2   veal loin chops

Mix together the soy sauce, sesame oil, garlic, ginger, and green onion in a small, flat dish large enough to hold the chops. Add the chops, turning to coat both sides, and let marinate for 30 minutes to 1 hour.

Broil or grill to desired degree of doneness.

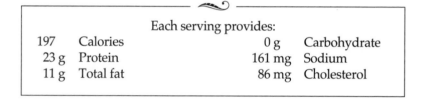

Each serving provides:			
197	Calories	0 g	Carbohydrate
23 g	Protein	161 mg	Sodium
11 g	Total fat	86 mg	Cholesterol

Wiener Schnitzel

It is important not to overcook the cutlets, or they will be dry and tough. A combination of oil and butter is used for sautéing—the butter adds flavor and the oil helps keep the butter from burning.

The cutlets should be served as soon as they are cooked. Serve with cooked noodles and freshly cooked spinach or a fresh green salad. A frosted stein of German beer would not be amiss!

Makes 4 servings

1	pound veal cutlets
2	egg whites
1	cup very fine dried bread crumbs
1	clove garlic, cut in half
1	tablespoon olive oil
2	teaspoons butter or margarine
4	thin slices lemon

Pound the cutlets well between two pieces of plastic wrap, then give them one or two more whacks for good measure.

In a small bowl, lightly beat the egg whites with 2 teaspoons water.

Place the bread crumbs on a flat plate. Dip a veal cutlet into the crumbs, then into the egg white mixture, then into the crumbs again. Lay cutlets on a rack and refrigerate, uncovered, for 30 minutes.

Rub a nonstick skillet with the cut side of the garlic. Over medium heat add the oil and butter and when heated, cook the cutlets, browning them carefully on both sides. Cook until tender. Top each cutlet with a slice of lemon.

Each serving provides:

395	Calories	19 g	Carbohydrate
41 g	Protein	318 mg	Sodium
16 g	Total fat	126 mg	Cholesterol

Veal Scallops with Orange Cream Sauce

We were going to call this "escalopes de veau a la crème l'orange," but the English translation works just as well.

Makes 3 servings

8	to 10 ounces veal scallops
	salt and pepper, to taste
1¹/₂	tablespoons olive oil
³/₄	cup sliced mushrooms (brush or peel, do not wash)
2	slices fresh ginger (size of quarters)
1	large clove garlic, sliced
¹/₂	cup orange juice
¹/₃	cup non-fat sour cream

Season veal with a light sprinkling of salt and pepper. Place the slices of veal well apart between two pieces of plastic wrap and pound slices until they are larger and thin. (If you don't have a meat mallet, the bottom of a cast-iron frying pan works well, as does an empty wine bottle.)

In a nonstick skillet, heat olive oil and sauté mushrooms over medium-high heat for about 5 minutes; transfer mushrooms to an oven-proof dish and keep warm in the oven. In the same skillet the mushrooms were cooked in, sauté the ginger and garlic for 3 minutes (this is just to flavor the oil, but it is an important step). Remove garlic and ginger with slotted spoon and discard.

In the same skillet over medium-high heat, sauté the veal slices on either side until cooked. This will take just a minute or two. Do not overcook, and work quickly. Place veal in a warm oven.

Add orange juice to skillet and boil over high heat until reduced to ¹/₃ cup, which should take 2 to 3 minutes. Remove pan from heat and stir in sour cream. Do not boil after sour cream has been added. Spoon sauce over meat and mushrooms and serve.

	Each serving provides:		
254	Calories	6 g	Carbohydrate
26 g	Protein	66 mg	Sodium
14 g	Total fat	95 mg	Cholesterol

Veal Rump Roast

Makes 6 to 8 servings

3	to 4 pounds veal rump roast
	salt and pepper, to taste
1¹/₂	cups apricot nectar
¹/₂	cup firmly packed brown sugar
1	grated orange rind
1	tablespoon orange juice
¹/₈	teaspoon cinnamon

Preheat oven to 325°. Season veal with salt and pepper and place on a rack in a shallow roasting pan. Roast for 1¹/₂ hours.

Meanwhile, make the apricot glaze: combine remaining ingredients in a small saucepan, bring to a boil, reduce heat, and simmer uncovered for 10 minutes, or until liquid has been reduced to a syrup or sauce-like consistency. Let cool.

After veal has roasted for 1¹/₂ hours, spoon a third of the apricot glaze over meat every 20 minutes. Bake until well done, about 2¹/₄ to 2¹/₂ hours total baking time or until a meat thermometer registers 170°.

Each serving provides:

298	Calories	21 g	Carbohydrate
34 g	Protein	116 mg	Sodium
8 g	Total fat	134 mg	Cholesterol

Moroccan Veal Stew

Bottom or top round steak may be substituted for the veal in this dish. Serve with a mixture of cooked wild rice and brown rice.

Makes 4 to 6 servings

4	tablespoons all-purpose flour
1^1/$_2$	teaspoons ground cumin
1^1/$_2$	teaspoons oregano
^{1}/$_4$	to ^{1}/$_2$ teaspoon salt
^{1}/$_2$	teaspoon ground allspice
^{1}/$_8$	teaspoon cayenne pepper
2	pounds lean veal stew meat, cut into 1-inch pieces and trimmed of any visible fat
2	tablespoons olive oil
^{1}/$_2$	can (5^1/$_2$ ounces) tomato paste
^{1}/$_2$	cup orange juice
1^1/$_2$	tablespoons red wine vinegar
1^1/$_2$	tablespoons brown sugar
^{1}/$_4$	teaspoon black pepper
2	cups mushrooms, cut into halves or quarters
1	large onion, peeled, cut into quarters, then slivered
2	cups sliced carrots

Preheat oven to 250°. Combine flour, cumin, oregano, salt, allspice, and cayenne pepper in a plastic bag. Add veal and shake well to coat.

Heat the olive oil in a nonstick heavy-bottom skillet and brown veal on all sides over medium heat. If veal starts to stick while browning, add a drop or two of water or stock, just enough to prevent sticking. Transfer veal to a large casserole and cover.

Stir any remaining seasoned flour into the skillet (there should be 1 tablespoon or less). Stir in ^{1}/$_2$ cup water and bring to a boil, scraping up any brown bits that may have stuck to the bottom of the pan. Stir in the tomato paste, then orange juice, vinegar, brown sugar, and black pepper. Bring to boil, stirring constantly, and pour over the meat in the casserole. Scrape all of the sauce out of the skillet and wipe skillet clean.

Spray skillet with nonstick cooking spray and lightly brown the mushrooms over medium heat (the best way to turn the mushrooms is to give the pan a good shake). Add mushrooms to casserole along with the onions and carrots. Stir to mix, then cover tightly and bake for 3 to 4 hours or until tender (check with a fork after 3 hours for tenderness).

Each serving provides:

315	Calories	25 g	Carbohydrate
34 g	Protein	384 mg	Sodium
9 g	Total fat	128 mg	Cholesterol

Osso Buco

Ask your butcher for veal shanks if you don't see them in the case. This method does not follow the traditional browning of the shanks in a mixture of butter and olive oil before saucing and baking; instead, the meat is slowly baked to release excess fat, which is then removed before a robust sauce is added. It is then finished in the oven.

If you're tempted to eat the delicious marrow inside the bones—don't. It is 25 to 35 percent animal fat. The rest of the dish, however, is lowfat, so enjoy!

Serve with saffron rice (or risotto) and Italian green beans. This popular Italian dish is often served with gremolata, which adds 1 teaspoon of finely minced garlic to the parsley and lemon rind garnish recipe below. Pass it separately to sprinkle over the top. The gremolata should be made just shortly before serving.

Makes 4 servings

Osso Buco

4	cross cut sections of veal shank, 2 inches thick (about 4 pounds total)
	salt and pepper, to taste
1	tablespoon olive oil
1^1/$_2$	cups finely minced onion
1^1/$_2$	cups diced carrot
1^1/$_2$	cups diced celery
3	tablespoons whole wheat flour
1	can (10 ounces) beef broth (see note)
1	cup red wine (see note)
2	tablespoons minced fresh parsley
^{1}/$_2$	can (can is 5^1/$_2$ ounces) tomato paste
1	teaspoon liquid Bovril or instant beef stock
^{1}/$_2$	teaspoon black pepper
1	bay leaf

Garnish

^{1}/$_2$	cup chopped fresh parsley
	grated rind of 1 lemon

Preheat oven to 275°. In a large casserole dish (or small roasting pan large enough to hold the veal shanks in one layer), arrange shanks and season with salt and pepper to taste. Roast meat, tightly covered, for 2 hours. Remove from oven and carefully pour off juices that have accumulated in the bottom. Skim fat off juices, but save juice.

While shanks are baking, heat olive oil in a skillet. Add onion and sauté over low heat until onion starts to soften. Stir in carrot and celery. Cover and continue to cook over low heat, allowing vegetables to "sweat."

When vegetables are soft, sprinkle with flour, then stir in beef broth, then red wine, parsley, tomato paste, Bovril, and pepper. Bring to a boil, stirring constantly, until thickened. Stir in any saved juices from the meat.

Pour vegetable mixture over shanks, then add bay leaf. Cover tightly and return to the oven for an additional 1 1/2 hours or until meat is tender.

Remove bay leaf. Serve garnished with chopped fresh parsley and lemon rind.

Note: The beef broth and red wine can be substituted with 1 can chicken broth and 1 cup white wine. This is particularly suitable if you are lucky enough to find the milk-fed provimi veal. Most North American veal, however, is grain-fed, making the beef broth and red wine our choice.

Each serving provides:			
161	Calories	24 g	Carbohydrate
6 g	Protein	960 mg	Sodium
4 g	Total fat	2 mg	Cholesterol

Veal Marsala

Once you have the ingredients assembled, this dish can be cooked and served in 10 minutes. The secret to the success of this dish is to work quickly.

Serve with orzo or penne pasta, fresh asparagus, and broiled tomato halves. The chopped parsley is a must, as the veal is quite colorless.

Makes 2 to 3 servings

6	veal scallops, 2 ounces each
1	to 2 tablespoons flour
2	tablespoons olive oil
	pepper, to taste
1	teaspoon unsalted butter
2	shallots, chopped, or 2 green onions
6	large mushrooms, thinly sliced (brush to clean but don't wash)
1/4	cup Marsala wine or red wine
1/4	cup chicken stock
	chopped fresh parsley

Place the slices of veal well apart between two pieces of plastic wrap and pound slices until they are large and thin. (If you don't have a meat mallet, use the bottom of a cast-iron frying pan or an empty wine bottle.) Lightly dredge veal with flour, shaking off any excess.

In a nonstick skillet, heat oil over medium-high heat and lightly brown one side of scallops, sprinkle with pepper, then brown 1 minute on other side. Work quickly and don't overcook. Remove scallops to a warm serving platter.

Add butter to the same pan and sauté the shallots and mushrooms until shallots are soft (if mushrooms start to stick, add a few drops of the chicken stock). Add wine and chicken stock to pan. Increase heat and boil rapidly, scraping the bottom, until liquid is slightly reduced. Spoon over top of scallops, sprinkle with chopped parsley, and serve immediately.

Each serving provides:

399	Calories	8 g	Carbohydrate
39 g	Protein	351 mg	Sodium
21 g	Total fat	143 mg	Cholesterol

Pasta

W as there life before pasta? Hard to imagine, isn't it? No longer is pasta considered just a fattening filler-food. More and more people are experimenting with the endless variety of shapes and sizes and are discovering which sauces best suit which types. Does a tomato sauce taste as good on fettucine as it does on spaghetti? Does the width of the pasta make a difference? You betcha!

Today we not only have a variety of shapes to choose from, but also colors: green, brown, orange, even black. (Don't even think of chocolate pasta!) Whole wheat pasta has more fiber, more vitamins, and more minerals than regular pasta, but it also has a stronger flavor. It is best to mix whole wheat with regular pasta if you are using it for the first time, just to get used to it.

One cup of cooked spaghetti or 1 1/2 cups of medium-sized macaroni contains only 1 gram of fat. Pasta also contains iron, riboflavin, niacin, and thiamine. Toss it with strips of cooked beef for protein and some vegetables for fiber. Follow this with a fresh fruit dessert, and you have a very healthy meal.

If you find you are cooking pasta fairly regularly, you should really invest in a pasta cooker (if you do not already own one). It is a large pot with a colander insert for draining the pasta.

Cooking Pasta

Packaged pasta, whether fresh or dried, always comes with cooking instructions. Follow the instructions carefully. Here are a few additional points to keep in mind while following our recipes.

- You wait for the pasta; pasta doesn't wait for you. So have your plates warm and the sauce ready.
- Use a very large pot and lots of water. The more water, the less chance of a gummy end result. Overcooking pasta will also make it gummy.
- Water must always be boiling when pasta is added.
- Add salt just before you add the pasta, and always cook without a lid.
- Fresh pasta cooks much faster than dried. Fresh pasta takes from 2 to 6 minutes, and dried pasta can take from 8 to 20 minutes, depending on the size and shape.

- Do not overcook! Begin testing pasta well before you think it is ready. Following suggested cooking times on the box isn't always reliable, because there are so many variables. Tasting the pasta is the best way to determine when it is done. When properly cooked, the pasta is slightly resilient to the bite (or al dente). At this stage, the pasta not only tastes best, but it also has the highest nutritional value.
- When the pasta is done, drain it immediately. Do not rinse in cold water unless it is to be used in a salad or unless the recipe specifically calls for it.
- Generally, 4 ounces of dried pasta is required per person.

Make-Ahead Party Casserole

Go ahead and make lots, but follow this recipe exactly as directed. Don't substitute anything for the sherry, don't alter the amount of pasta, and don't cut down on the garlic (yes, 6 cloves).

Makes 8 to 10 servings

1¹/₄	cups small-size pasta shells
2	pounds extra-lean ground beef
3	medium onions, finely chopped
6	cloves garlic, minced
1	green pepper, seeded and diced
1	can (28 ounces) diced tomatoes
1	can (14 ounces) corn niblets, drained
1	can (10 ounces) mushrooms, drained
1	cup lowfat cheddar cheese, diced fairly small
1	tablespoon brown sugar
2	teaspoons chili powder
3	tablespoons Worcestershire sauce
1	teaspoon black pepper
¹/₂	cup sherry

Cook pasta shells, rinse with cold water, and set aside.

Over medium-high heat, sauté beef in a very large nonstick skillet or Dutch oven, breaking up with a wooden spoon, until all trace of pink disappears. Drain any accumulated fat. Add onions, garlic, and green pepper, mix well, and cook until vegetables soften, about 5 minutes.

In your largest casserole, combine tomatoes, corn niblets, mushrooms, cheese, brown sugar, chili powder, Worcestershire sauce, pepper, and sherry. Stir in cooked shells and beef mixture. Place in refrigerator for several hours (can be overnight).

When ready to cook, preheat oven to 350°. Bake casserole for
1 hour or until hot and bubbly.

Note: An additional $1/2$ cup grated cheese may be sprinkled over
the top of the casserole before baking.

Each serving provides:

372	Calories	30 g	Carbohydrate
28 g	Protein	403 mg	Sodium
16 g	Total fat	73 mg	Cholesterol

Jane's Spaghetti Sauce

Jane has been making this sauce for years, but occasionally she would experiment with a new sauce, which never failed to incite threats of mutiny from her husband (a judge) and her four children.

Makes 6 to 8 servings

1	medium onion, chopped
1	clove garlic, minced
1¹/₂	pounds extra-lean ground beef
2	cans (19 ounces each) tomatoes
1	can (7¹/₂ ounces) tomato sauce
³/₄	cup ketchup
¹/₄	cup white vinegar
¹/₈	cup Worcestershire sauce
³/₄	teaspoon Tabasco
1	tablespoon brown sugar
2	teaspoons thyme
1	teaspoon no-salt seasoning (page 260) or ¹/₂ teaspoon no-salt seasoning and ¹/₂ teaspoon salt
	sprinkling of cayenne pepper
1	pound spaghetti

Spray Dutch oven with nonstick cooking spray and cook onion over medium heat until it starts to brown. Add garlic and meat and cook, breaking up meat with a fork until no trace of pink remains in the meat. Add tomatoes, tomato sauce, ketchup, vinegar, Worcestershire sauce, Tabasco, brown sugar, thyme, salt, and cayenne pepper, breaking up tomatoes with a fork. Simmer for 30 minutes.

Cook spaghetti in a large amount of boiling well-salted water until al dente. Drain and toss with sauce.

Each serving provides:			
503	Calories	64 g	Carbohydrate
26 g	Protein	780 mg	Sodium
16 g	Total fat	59 mg	Cholesterol

Cantonese Beef and Noodles

Making this dish is also a good way to deal with a bit of leftover beef. Substitute leftover beef cut into thin strips for the steak.

This recipe serves four people if you're serving it with one additional dish. If it's a main dish, it will serve three people (or two people who are power-dining).

Makes 4 servings

8	ounces vermicelli or spaghettini
1	pound lean steak (tenderloin or sirloin)
2	tablespoons canola oil or safflower oil
2	large cloves garlic, minced
1¹/₂	tablespoon peeled and finely slivered fresh ginger
10	green onions, cut into 1¹/₂-inch lengths
2	tablespoons oyster sauce (see note)
4	teaspoons rice wine vinegar (see note)
²/₃	cup beef broth
1	teaspoon sugar
1	teaspoon sesame oil

Cook vermicelli in a large amount of boiling well-salted water until al dente. Rinse with cold water, drain, and set aside.

Cut steak into small narrow strips (this is easier to do if steak is partially frozen). Heat oil in large nonstick skillet or wok. Add beef strips and stir-fry over medium-high heat until all trace of pink disappears from the surface of the meat. You want the meat to be rare at this point.

Stir in garlic, ginger, and green onions and continue to stir-fry for 30 to 60 seconds. Add oyster sauce, rice wine vinegar, beef broth, sugar, and sesame oil. Stir until well mixed.

Add pasta to wok. Toss mixture (best to use a wooden spoon and a fork for this) until pasta is well heated through.

Note: Oyster sauce and rice wine vinegar are available in the Asian section of most supermarkets.

Each serving provides:

450	Calories	51 g	Carbohydrate
27 g	Protein	524 mg	Sodium
15 g	Total fat	54 mg	Cholesterol

Helen's Meat Rolls with Spaghetti

This recipe is well worth the time and effort spent in making it.

Makes 8 servings

Filling
1¹/₂	cups seedless raisins
¹/₂	cup blanched almonds
¹/₂	cup chopped celery
¹/₂	cup chopped onion
¹/₄	cup grated Parmesan cheese
1	egg, lightly beaten
¹/₂	teaspoon salt

Meat Rolls
8	minute steaks, trimmed of all visible fat
¹/₄	cup flour
¹/₂	teaspoon pepper
¹/₄	teaspoon paprika
2	tablespoons olive oil
¹/₂	cup chopped onion
1	clove garlic, minced
1	can (28 ounces) tomatoes
1	can (7¹/₂ ounces) tomato sauce
¹/₂	teaspoon salt
¹/₂	teaspoon sweet basil

Additional
1	pound spaghetti

Grind raisins and almonds together through fine blade of food chopper.

Spray a nonstick skillet with nonstick cooking spray; add celery and onion. Cook gently over medium-low heat, stirring often, for 5 minutes (if it starts to stick, add a drop or two of water or vegetable or beef stock). Add raisins and almonds; cover and cook gently for an additional 2 to 3 minutes. Remove from heat and cool.

Stir Parmesan cheese, egg, and salt into the raisin mixture and blend well.

Lay minute steaks on a table or flat surface and divide raisin mixture evenly among them. Spread mixture to within ¹/₄ inch of the edge of the steaks and roll up the steaks in a jelly roll-fashion, tying each with string.

Combine flour, $1/4$ teaspoon of the pepper, and paprika and roll each steak in the mixture.

Heat olive oil in a large nonstick skillet and brown steaks on all sides over medium-high heat. Remove steaks as they brown and set aside. Add onion and garlic to pan drippings. Cook gently over low heat for 5 minutes. Add tomatoes (breaking up with a fork), tomato sauce, salt, remaining $1/4$ teaspoon of the pepper, and sweet basil and simmer for 5 minutes.

Return meat rolls to pan, cover, and simmer gently, turning rolls frequently, for about 1 hour or until meat is tender.

Cook spaghetti in a large amount of boiling well-salted water until al dente. Drain thoroughly.

Lift meat rolls out of sauce and remove strings. Put in center of a large serving plate. Surround meat with hot cooked spaghetti. Pour sauce over all. Pass additional Parmesan cheese if desired.

Each serving provides:

604	Calories	80 g	Carbohydrate
40 g	Protein	749 mg	Sodium
15 g	Total fat	94 mg	Cholesterol

Lasagne

After cooking, wait 15 to 20 minutes before serving to let the lasagne settle. It will cut and serve better.

Makes 8 servings

9	lasagne noodles
2	tablespoons olive oil
1	medium onion, finely chopped
1	clove garlic, minced
1	pound extra-lean ground beef
1	can (10 ounces) sliced mushrooms (save the liquid)
1	can (8 ounces) tomato sauce
1	can (5$1/2$ ounces) tomato paste
$1/2$	teaspoon salt
1	teaspoon dried oregano
1	piece of peeled ginger, about 1 inch thick
1	egg
1	package (10 ounces) frozen chopped spinach, thawed and drained
1	cup lowfat ricotta or cottage cheese
$1/3$	cup grated Parmesan cheese
1	package (8 ounces) lowfat mozzarella cheese, grated or thinly sliced

Preheat oven to 350°. Cook lasagne noodles according to package directions, drain, then hold in cold water until ready to use.

In a large saucepan, heat 1 tablespoon of the olive oil and sauté onion and garlic over medium heat; add beef and brown. Drain off any fat. Stir in mushrooms (including liquid), tomato sauce, tomato paste, salt, oregano, $3/4$ cup water, and ginger. Simmer for 15 minutes. Remove piece of ginger and discard.

Mix egg with spinach, ricotta cheese, Parmesan cheese, and remaining 1 tablespoon of olive oil. Spread one-third of the meat sauce in bottom of a 9 × 13-inch baking dish. Place 3 cooked noodles on top and spread with an additional one-third of the sauce. Place 3 more cooked noodles on top. Spread with spinach-cheese mixture. Cover with remaining noodles and spread with remaining sauce. Arrange mozzarella cheese on top and bake for 35 to 40 minutes.

Each serving provides:

463	Calories	40 g	Carbohydrate
33 g	Protein	1041 mg	Sodium
20 g	Total fat	91 mg	Cholesterol

Tenderloin Strips with Roasted Garlic and Sun-Dried Tomato Sauce

We like to use elephant garlic for this dish, but if you can't find it, use regular garlic. You can also stretch one steak to serve two people. This sauce is so good, it can stand on its own without the steak!

Serve with tossed green salad and cheese toast.

Makes 2 servings

Sauce

2	tablespoons soft margarine
2	tablespoons flour
2	teaspoons beef bouillon granules
1	can (13 ounces) 2 percent evaporated canned milk
1/2	teaspoon salt
1/4	teaspoon black pepper
1/4	teaspoon dried basil
1	tablespoon tomato paste

Tenderloin Strips

1	tenderloin steak, 8 to 10 ounces, sliced thinly (best to do this when partially frozen)
2	tablespoons roasted garlic, minced and mashed (see note)
2	tablespoons slivered sun-dried tomatoes

Additional

1/2	pound hot cooked linguine or pasta of your choice

Melt the margarine in a small saucepan over low heat. Stir in flour and bouillon granules. Gradually stir in the evaporated milk, salt, pepper, basil, and tomato paste. Cook over medium heat, stirring constantly, until the sauce thickens, about 3 to 5 minutes. Set aside while you cook the steak.

Sauté the beef quickly over high heat, but don't spoil the tenderloin by overcooking. Stir into the sauce along with the roasted garlic and sun-dried tomatoes. When well heated through, remove from heat, spoon over cooked pasta, and serve.

Note: To roast garlic, rub unpeeled cloves of elephant garlic with olive oil, sprinkle lightly with salt, wrap in foil, and roast in the center of a 350° oven for 45 to 60 minutes or until soft. Let cool. If you are using regular garlic, use 1 large head and separate, removing outer layer of skin but leaving peel on cloves. Place in shallow small roasting pan and toss with 1 tablespoon olive oil and a light sprinkle of salt; wrap in foil and roast, until cloves are soft (start checking after 40 minutes). Squeeze skins to release soft pulp.

Each serving provides:			
650	Calories	64 g	Carbohydrate
44 g	Protein	1850 mg	Sodium
22 g	Total fat	102 mg	Cholesterol

Veal Balls in Italian Sauce
with Oven-Dried Grapes

*Make the oven-dried grapes a day or two ahead. They add a definite interest
to the dish. They look like very large raisins but have quite a different flavor.*

Makes 4 to 6 servings

Sauce

2	tablespoons olive oil
2	cloves garlic, minced
1	teaspoon dried basil
1	teaspoon dried mint
1/2	teaspoon dried oregano
1/4	teaspoon dried crushed red pepper
1/4	teaspoon freshly ground black pepper
1	can (28 ounces) diced tomatoes
1	can (5 1/2 ounces) tomato paste plus 1 can water

Veal Balls

1/2	pound lean ground veal (or substitute lean ground beef)
2	tablespoons fine dry bread crumbs
2	tablespoons lowfat milk
1	egg white, lightly beaten
1	teaspoon finely chopped parsley
1/8	teaspoon salt
1/4	teaspoon black pepper
2	tablespoons chopped fresh parsley
2	tablespoons sugar
1/2	cup dried grapes (see note)
1	can (10 ounces) button mushrooms, drained
1	small green pepper, seeded and diced into fairly large pieces

Additional

1	package (16 ounces) spaghettini or vermicelli, cooked

In a large, heavy skillet, on low heat, very slowly heat the oil, garlic, basil, mint, oregano, crushed red pepper, and black pepper. Let
cook for about 5 minutes, or until garlic is golden. Don't let garlic
burn, or sauce will be bitter.

Turn heat up and add tomatoes, and tomato paste and water. Bring to a boil. Reduce heat and simmer, covered, for 25 minutes, stirring occasionally.

Meanwhile, make the meatballs: put the ground veal, bread crumbs, milk, egg white, parsley, salt, and pepper in a bowl and mix thoroughly. Shape into small balls, about 1/2 inch in diameter. Spray a nonstick skillet with nonstick cooking spray and brown meatballs over medium-high heat, turning to brown evenly (give the pan a good shake to turn the balls nicely). Drain off any fat.

To the sauce, add parsley, sugar, dried grapes, mushrooms, green pepper, and meatballs and continue to simmer, uncovered, for an additional 20 minutes, stirring occasionally. Don't overcook the green peppers; you want them to still have a bit of snap to them.

Serve over hot cooked spaghettini or vermicelli.

Note: Make oven-dried grapes the day before you will be cooking with them. Wash 1 cup seedless red grapes, dry, and place in a 200° oven for 6 hours. You don't want them dried and pliable like a sun-dried tomato; the grapes should still be a little soft in the center. One cup of fresh grapes yields 1/2 cup dried grapes.

Each serving provides:			
506	Calories	85 g	Carbohydrate
22 g	Protein	718 mg	Sodium
9 g	Total fat	34 mg	Cholesterol

Pasta and Meatballs with
Sun-Dried Tomato Sauce

This dish can be served over any pasta of your choice. Try the currently popular penne pasta.

Makes 4 servings

Meatballs
1   pound lean ground beef
1   egg white, lightly beaten
$1/4$ cup dry bread crumbs
$1/4$ cup pine nuts, coarsely chopped (leave some whole)
$1/3$ cup finely chopped green onions
$1/4$ cup black currants
$1/4$ teaspoon salt
$1/2$ teaspoon dried crushed red pepper flakes
2   cloves garlic, minced

Sauce
$1/3$ cup sun-dried tomatoes
1   medium to large red onion, finely chopped
1   green pepper, seeded and diced
1   large tomato, diced
4   tablespoons tomato paste
1   can (10 ounces) Italian-style tomato soup
$1/2$ cup red wine
3   tablespoons chopped fresh basil, or 1 teaspoon dried basil
$1/4$ teaspoon black pepper
1   teaspoon brown sugar

Additional
1   pound pasta

Preheat oven to 450°. Combine ground beef, egg white, bread crumbs, pine nuts, green onions, currants, salt, red pepper flakes, and garlic in a medium-size bowl. Mix well with wet hands and shape into $1^1/2$-inch balls (you should have about 22 balls). Spray a cookie sheet with nonstick cooking spray, arrange meatballs on the sheet, and bake for 12 to 15 minutes.

Reconstitute the sun-dried tomatoes by placing in boiling water; boil for 2 minutes or until soft. Drain and chop coarsely. Discard water (or save to add to a soup).

To make the sauce, spray a large saucepan or Dutch oven with nonstick cooking spray and sauté the onion and green pepper over medium heat until soft. Add tomato, tomato paste, tomato soup, red wine, 1/2 cup water, basil, pepper, and brown sugar and bring to a boil.

When meatballs are done, drain and add to the sauce. Add sun-dried tomatoes. Let mixture simmer gently, covered, for 25 to 30 minutes.

Cook pasta in a large amount of boiling well-salted water until al dente; drain.

Serve sauce over hot cooked pasta.

Each serving provides:

728	Calories	90 g	Carbohydrate
41 g	Protein	940 mg	Sodium
23 g	Total fat	81 mg	Cholesterol

Orange Beef

It's hard to put a label on this dish. It's not Italian or Chinese (maybe Ital-Asian?). The meat is not marinated or tenderized, so use good top sirloin and slice thinly (which is a cinch when the meat is partially frozen).
Serve with Doreen's Special Salad (page 251).

Makes 4 to 5 servings

1	tablespoon olive oil
12	medium-size mushrooms, sliced (brush or peel, but don't wash)
2	medium onions, thinly sliced
1	pound top sirloin steak, thinly sliced on an angle grated rind of 1 orange
1	tablespoon liquid Bovril or instant beef stock
3	tablespoons orange juice concentrate
1	cup orange juice
1	teaspoon ground ginger
1	tablespoon molasses
1/4	teaspoon dried crushed red pepper
12	ounces broad noodles, cooked chopped fresh parsley

Heat the oil in a large skillet. Cook the mushrooms and onions over very low heat. When onions are translucent, add the sliced beef and cook very gently until most of the pink disappears from the beef.

Combine the orange rind, Bovril, orange juice concentrate, orange juice, ginger, molasses, and crushed red pepper in a small saucepan and heat. Add to beef. Simmer gently for about 10 minutes. Make sure the mixture doesn't get too hot and toughens the meat.

Spoon beef mixture over top of hot cooked noodles in a large, shallow serving dish. Sprinkle with chopped fresh parsley.

Each serving provides:

544	Calories	70 g	Carbohydrate
36 g	Protein	349 mg	Sodium
13 g	Total fat	134 mg	Cholesterol

Leftovers

L ove is lovelier the second time around, but how about beef? Try the recipes in this chapter and decide for yourself. You will find many innovative ways to deal with your leftover roast, and all of them are delicious.

Leftover beef can be a time-saver. It can be sliced for hot or cold sandwiches, cubed for casseroles and skillet dishes, or cut into strips for stir-fries, salads, pizzas, or stroganoffs.

Try beef in a pita. Combine 2 tablespoons lowfat mayonnaise with 1 teaspoon horseradish and spread inside pita halves. Fill each half with thinly sliced red onion, sliced roast beef, and fresh lettuce or sprouts. Another filling for pita can be made by increasing the mayonnaise and adding some chopped green onion, celery, and a bit of sweet pickle relish before mixing in some strips of cold roast beef. Spoon filling into pita bread pockets and top with some shredded lettuce.

Beef on a bagel is another treat to enjoy with leftover roast beef (rare is best). Combine 1 tablespoon lite cream cheese with a dash or two of Worcestershire sauce and spread on a bagel half. Top with several slices of cooked roast beef and garnish with chopped green onion. Microwave on medium for 1 to $1^1/2$ minutes or until warm.

Roast Beef Blintzes

Makes 8 servings

1	cup mashed potatoes
1	cup cooked, ground leftover lean roast beef
	seasoned salt, to taste
	pepper, to taste
1	to 2 tablespoons fried chopped onions (see note)
8	crepes (can use ready-made for convenience)
	non-fat sour cream

Preheat oven to 350°. Combine the potatoes, beef, salt, pepper, and fried onions. Shape into cylinders and roll in crepes, tucking in the ends as you roll. Each crepe should hold about 1/4 cup of the filling mixture. Place crepes in a baking dish sprayed with nonstick cooking spray and bake until heated through, about 20 minutes.

Serve 2 per person and top with sour cream.

Note: When frying the onions, use a nonstick skillet, spray with nonstick cooking spray and use only 1 teaspoon butter.

Each serving provides:

117	Calories	10 g	Carbohydrate
11 g	Protein	221 mg	Sodium
3 g	Total fat	65 mg	Cholesterol

Chinese Beef with Broccoli

This is best with leftover roast tenderloin. You want the beef tender and a bit on the rare side. You could also use eye of the round.

Makes 3 to 4 servings

1/2	cup oyster sauce (available in the Asian food section of super-markets)
3	tablespoons sherry
1	tablespoon cornstarch
1/4	teaspoon dried crushed red pepper
2	tablespoons canola oil
1	tablespoon fine julienne of fresh ginger
1	clove garlic, minced
3	cups small fresh broccoli florets
1	sweet red pepper, seeded and cut into strips
2	celery stalks, cut diagonally
1	cup diagonally sliced green onion
2	cups leftover roast beef, preferably rare or medium rare, cut into thin narrow strips
3	tablespoons chopped fresh Chinese parsley, optional

Place oyster sauce, 1/4 cup water, sherry, and cornstarch in a small bowl and stir until cornstarch is dissolved. Stir in crushed red pepper. Set aside.

Heat oil in a large nonstick skillet or wok and stir-fry ginger and garlic over medium heat for 30 seconds. Add broccoli and stir-fry for 3 minutes. Turn heat to high and stir in red pepper, celery, and green onion and continue to stir-fry for an additional 3 minutes. Stir in oyster sauce mixture and beef and stir constantly until mixture thickens, 2 to 3 minutes. Sprinkle parsley over top (optional). Serve with rice.

Each serving provides:

301	Calories	15 g	Carbohydrate
30 g	Protein	1314 mg	Sodium
12 g	Total fat	69 mg	Cholesterol

Creamy, Crunchy Salad

This is a perfect light meal for a hot summer night. Add good French bread and perhaps a fresh fruit dessert.

As a main course, this recipe serves four people; as a side dish, it serves eight to ten people.

Makes 4 servings

Salad
1   cup cold roast beef, preferably medium rare, cut into slivers
1   cup frozen peas (see note)
1   cup chopped mild onion
1   cup chopped celery
1/2   cup raisins
1/2   cup small cauliflower florets
1/2   cup tiny broccoli florets
1/4   cup chopped carrot

Salad Dressing
1   cup ranch-style salad dressing
1/2   cup non-fat sour cream

Combine the roast beef, peas, onion, celery, raisins, cauliflower, broccoli, and carrot in a large bowl.

Combine salad dressing and sour cream well in a small bowl. Toss salad with the dressing.

Note: If you plan to serve the salad right away, let peas thaw at room temperature. Drain on paper towels, then add to rest of vegetables. Serve salad the day it is prepared.

Each serving provides:			
424	Calories	32 g	Carbohydrate
20 g	Protein	506 mg	Sodium
26 g	Total fat	51 mg	Cholesterol

Curried Roast Beef

This is an excellent dish for utilizing leftover beef. Serve with hot, fluffy rice, condiments of your choice, and Doreen's Special Salad (page 251).

Makes 4 to 6 servings

Curry
1	tablespoon olive oil
1	large onion, cut into 4 wedges, then thinly sliced
3	cloves garlic, minced
2	rounded tablespoons curry powder
1	tablespoon cumin
$1/4$	teaspoon Tabasco
2	cups beef broth
2	tablespoons tomato paste
1	small to medium sweet red pepper, chopped
3	to 4 cups cooked beef, diced
1	small apple, diced
2	tablespoons flour
2	tablespoons sherry
$1/4$	cup raisins

Suggested Condiments
raisins or currants (nice plumped in sherry or brandy)
chopped green onion
mango chutney (chop any large pieces)
chopped ripe tomatoes (Roma tomatoes work well)
chopped banana
chopped candied ginger
chopped green or red pepper

In a nonstick, heavy-bottom pan or Dutch oven, heat the oil and sauté the onion and garlic over medium-high heat. Stir in curry powder and cumin and let these spices "fry" a little with the onion and garlic. Stir in hot sauce, beef broth, and tomato paste; when smooth, stir in the red pepper and beef. Turn down the heat and simmer, covered, very gently for about 20 minutes. Add the apple and simmer for an additional 10 minutes.

Shake the flour and sherry together in a small jar until smooth, then stir into curry along with the raisins. Simmer for an additional 5 minutes.

Note: If you prefer a hotter curry, at the end of cooking add cayenne pepper, starting with $1/8$ teaspoon until you reach the desired heat level.

Each serving provides:

245	Calories	15 g	Carbohydrate
27 g	Protein	381 mg	Sodium
8 g	Total fat	69 mg	Cholesterol

Leftover Roast Beef Casserole

Makes 4 to 6 servings

3	to 4 cups leftover lean roast beef, cut into cubes
1	can (14 ounces) tomatoes
1	package onion soup mix
1	can (4 ounces) baked beans (see note)
1	can (7½ ounces) tomato sauce
⅛	to ¼ teaspoon garlic powder
¼	teaspoon oregano
2	onions, peeled and diced into large pieces
2	large carrots, peeled and diced

Preheat oven to 350°. Combine the beef, tomatoes, soup mix, baked beans, tomato sauce, garlic powder, oregano, onions, and carrots in a casserole dish. Bake, covered, for 1 hour.

If, after an hour, the casserole is a little too soupy, stir and bake for an additional ½ hour, uncovered.

Note: Try to find beans baked without pork; if not, remove any visible pieces.

Each serving provides:

254	Calories	23 g	Carbohydrate
29 g	Protein	1094 mg	Sodium
6 g	Total fat	69 mg	Cholesterol

Beef in Tortillas

*The beef is served wrapped in warm tortillas, but you can also put the mix-
ture in a taco shell, with salsa and non-fat sour cream for garnishing.*

Makes 6 servings

1¹/2	teaspoons vegetable oil
1¹/2	cups sliced onions
1	clove garlic, minced
1¹/2	cups diced zucchini
1¹/2	cups chopped fresh tomatoes
1	can (7¹/2 ounces) tomato sauce
1	teaspoon apple cider vinegar
¹/3	teaspoon sugar
¹/3	teaspoon salt
¹/3	teaspoon chili powder
	pinch of cumin
	pinch of curry powder
¹/8	teaspoon dried crushed red pepper
1	cup julienne strips of cooked roast beef, preferably medium rare
8	to 10 flour tortillas

Heat oil in a nonstick skillet over medium heat and stir-fry the
onions, garlic, and zucchini until tender-crisp. Stir in tomatoes,
tomato sauce, vinegar, sugar, salt, chili powder, cumin, curry powder,
and chili peppers. As soon as mixture comes to a boil, stir in the beef
and continue to cook just until the beef is well heated through. Wrap
in warmed tortillas and serve.

	Each serving provides:		
254	Calories	35 g	Carbohydrate
16 g	Protein	466 mg	Sodium
6 g	Total fat	30 mg	Cholesterol

Bella's Rice Noodle Dish

Actually, Bella's original recipe has nothing to do with leftover beef (Bella is a marvelous cook who probably doesn't even eat leftovers). Her recipe calls for a whole fresh chicken breast cut up and sautéed with the garlic until golden brown, adding soy sauce and cooking until little beads of oil surface. But the recipe is the same once you start adding the vegetables.

This dish must include the rice noodles, which can be found in the Asian food section of most supermarkets.

Makes 3 to 4 servings

1	package (8 ounces) rice noodles (rice vermicelli)
1	tablespoon vegetable oil
1	large clove garlic, minced
3	tablespoons soy sauce
1	cup sliced carrots
1	cup sliced celery
1	cup sliced fresh green beans
2	cups sliced cabbage
2	cups julienne strips of cooked roast beef, preferably medium rare freshly ground black pepper

In a large bowl, cover rice noodles with cold water and soak for 30 minutes or until softened. Drain noodles.

While noodles are soaking, heat oil and garlic in a large saucepan or Dutch oven over medium-high heat. When garlic starts to sizzle, add soy sauce. Let boil for 10 seconds, then stir in carrots, celery, green beans, cabbage, and beef. Cook, stirring frequently, until vegetables are tender-crisp, about 10 minutes.

Add 1 1/2 cups water to this mixture. When it comes to a boil, add the rice noodles. Mix in and cook over medium heat until water is absorbed. Sprinkle with freshly ground black pepper and serve.

Each serving provides:

360	Calories	58 g	Carbohydrate
17 g	Protein	865 mg	Sodium
6 g	Total fat	35 mg	Cholesterol

Accompaniments

Most of the recipes in this chapter involve lowfat vegetables that complement beef and a few salads that are suitable as well. You might find new ideas in this section when you are stuck designing a menu for your new healthy lifestyle.

When cooking vegetables other than root vegetables, use methods that require only a small amount of liquid or none at all, such as steaming or cooking in the microwave. Stir-frying works best using nonstick skillets sprayed with nonstick cooking spray; if vegetables stick, add a small amount of stock or vegetable juice instead of oil or butter. Have the water boiling before you add root vegetables. It is important to retain as much of the nutrient value in your vegetables as possible. Today's studies show a stronger link between vitamins and nutrients and better health.

Onions are a perfect accompaniment to beef. Did you know that a medium-size onion has only 38 calories and makes a fine vegetable when simply roasted in the oven in its skin? It takes 5 to 10 minutes longer than a baked potato. Make sure you put onions in a pan or on a cookie sheet, as they tend to ooze a tiny bit. Peel off the outer skin before serving. Onions are a good source of calcium, vitamins A and C, and several B vitamins. They are also thought to contain an anticoagulant that may be very helpful in preventing heart disease. Anyway you slice 'em, they have to be a good deal!

Potatoes are a natural accompaniment to beef, so this chapter offers several different ways of preparing them.

When cooking with mushrooms, select fresh, firm mushrooms. Don't wash them, as they retain water and the vegetable dish won't be as good. Either brush with a mushroom brush, wipe, or peel if necessary.

Peas go great with roast beef. Fresh sweet peas from the garden need no help other than cooking to perfection (although even overcooking doesn't seem to ruin them for they are so good!). When you are looking for something to jazz up frozen peas, try stirring 1/4 cup mint jelly into the cooked peas. Don't overcook frozen peas—cook only until they start to dimple when you blow on them.

Tomatoes are another good accompaniment to beef, and they are so useful when designing a meal. To bring out the flavor in a simple baked or broiled tomato half, sprinkle the cut surfaces with celery salt and a pinch of sugar just before placing in the oven or under the broiler (this is one of those little tips passed on from mother to daughter before cookbooks became a staple in every kitchen).

And while we are on the subject of tips passed from one generation to the next, Grandmother claimed that a little brown sugar takes the "burp" out of turnips. Try spiking puree of turnip with a little horseradish. It's an excellent vegetable with roasts.

Bagel Chips

This recipe is a good way to utilize 1- to 2-day-old bagels. It's good with dips and spreads and as a soup accompaniment

Makes 5 to 6 chips per bagel

bagels
Garlic Plus (see note)

Preheat oven to 400°. Slice bagels crossways very thinly. Spray with nonstick cooking spray very sparingly on both sides. Sprinkle with Garlic Plus. Place on a cookie sheet and bake for 10 minutes. Watch carefully so that they don't burn.

Note: Garlic Plus, a mixture of garlic, spices, and seasonings, is a new product put out by Schilling (in the U.S.) and McCormick (in Canada). You will find it a useful flavoring agent but can substitute it with garlic powder.

Garlic-flavored cooking sprays are now available in most markets and can be used in place of the nonstick cooking spray and Garlic Plus in this recipe.

	Each chip provides:		
29	Calories	5 g	Carbohydrate
1 g	Protein	87 mg	Sodium
0 g	Total fat	0 mg	Cholesterol

Broiled Peaches

Makes 3 to 4 servings

1	can (19 ounces) cling peaches, drained
16	to 20 whole cloves
2	teaspoons brown sugar
2	teaspoons vinegar

Preheat oven to 350°. Place drained peach halves in shallow baking dish. Stick with a few cloves and sprinkle each half with 1/4 teaspoon brown sugar. Add 1/4 teaspoon vinegar to each peach half cavity and bake for 15 minutes or place under broiler until well-heated through.

Each serving provides:

69	Calories	18 g	Carbohydrate
1 g	Protein	6 mg	Sodium
0 g	Total fat	0 mg	Cholesterol

Louise's Popovers

Here's a logical question from one of the children: "Why aren't these called pop-uppers? They don't pop over—they pop up!"

Roast prime rib with its traditional Yorkshire pudding did not fit the objective of this book. However, you can still enjoy a wonderful roast of beef dinner with a tenderloin, sirloin tip, rump, or eye of the round roast, and the following popovers are a pretty good substitute for the Yorkshire pudding.

Makes 8 popovers

3	eggs, room temperature
$1/2$	teaspoon salt
1	cup 2 percent milk
1	cup flour

Spray Teflon muffin tins with nonstick cooking spray. Whisk the eggs and salt lightly. Add the milk and flour, mixing just until blended. Don't overmix (don't worry if it comes out a little lumpy).

Fill the pans half full. Place into a cold oven. Set oven to 425° and bake for 20 minutes. Reduce oven temperature to 375° and bake for an additional 10 to 15 minutes or until the popovers are golden brown and crisp on top. Turn oven off. Pierce each popover with a skewer to release steam and let popovers sit in closed oven for an additional 2 to 3 minutes.

Note: If you want larger popovers, use custard cups or a giant-size muffin pan. You will get 6 large-size popovers.

Each serving provides:			
101	Calories	14 g	Carbohydrate
5 g	Protein	173 mg	Sodium
3 g	Total fat	83 mg	Cholesterol

Carrot Bundles

These are very impressive at a dinner party. They can be assembled ahead of time and heated just at serving. When you're cutting the carrots, try to have them all the same length, so they'll look nicer.

Makes 4 servings

4   medium-sized carrots, cut into julienne strips, about 3 inches
1   green onion
1/2   to 1 teaspoon butter

Parboil carrots until tender-crisp. Remove white part of green onion and discard. Blanche the green onion stem, then cut into 4 long strips. Wrap strips around small bundles of carrots and tie in a knot. Set in a baking dish. Dot each bundle with 1/8 to 1/4 teaspoon butter. At serving time, microwave for 3 to 4 minutes or until heated through.

Each serving provides:

36	Calories	8 g	Carbohydrate
1 g	Protein	31 mg	Sodium
1 g	Total fat	1 mg	Cholesterol

Steamed Green Beans

Because the beans are cooked quickly, the nutrients aren't all leached out.
The garlic and soy sauce give a little extra flavor and interest without
adding any fat.

Makes 4 servings

1/2	cup low-salt chicken stock
1	tablespoon soy sauce
1	large clove garlic, peeled and thinly sliced
1	pound fresh green beans, trimmed and cut in half

Place chicken stock, soy sauce, and garlic in a 12-inch skillet. Bring
to a boil. Add green beans and cook, covered, over moderately high
heat for 4 minutes. Remove cover and cook until water is evaporated
and green beans are bright green and tender-crisp.

Each serving provides:

46	Calories	10 g	Carbohydrate
3 g	Protein	272 mg	Sodium
0 g	Total fat	0 mg	Cholesterol

Onions (Slightly Intoxicated)

This is a great dish to serve with beef. It can be made ahead and reheated in the microwave.

Makes 6 to 8 servings

4	medium to large onions, peeled and cut into $1/2$-inch slices
$1/4$	cup plus 2 tablespoons dry vermouth
4	tablespoons maple syrup
	pinch of cloves
$1/8$	teaspoon salt
1	tablespoon flour
1	teaspoon paprika

Place onions, $1/4$ cup of the vermouth, 2 tablespoons of the maple syrup, cloves, and salt in a medium saucepan with a tight-fitting lid. Bring to a boil. When steam starts escaping from under lid, you will know it is boiling without having to lift the lid; reduce heat to simmer and cook until soft, about 20 minutes.

Place flour, remaining 2 tablespoons of the vermouth, remaining 2 tablespoons of the maple syrup, and paprika in a small jar and shake well until free of lumps, then stir into onions until mixture starts to thicken. This will take only a matter of minutes.

Each serving provides:			
76	Calories	16 g	Carbohydrate
1 g	Protein	35 mg	Sodium
0 g	Total fat	0 mg	Cholesterol

Mushroom and Green Pepper Stir-Fry

Serving interesting vegetables is sometimes a bit of a challenge. Any vegetable is good when slathered in butter, but having no butter on vegetables forces us to be a bit more creative, especially when cooking for friends. Try the following combination with a filet roast of beef or a perfectly barbecued steak.

Makes 4 servings

1	tablespoon plus 1 teaspoon olive oil
1/2	cup sliced green onion
1	pound fresh mushrooms, halved (brush or wipe, but don't wash)
2	medium green peppers, seeded and cut into 1-inch pieces
1/3	cup brown sugar
2	tablespoons Dijon mustard
2	tablespoons Worcestershire sauce
1/4	cup red wine
1/4	teaspoon black pepper

Heat oil in large skillet. Add green onion and cook until onion starts to soften. Add mushrooms and green peppers and cook over medium heat, stirring often, until mushrooms start to brown (this will take only 2 to 3 minutes). Remove from heat.

Combine brown sugar, Dijon mustard, Worcestershire sauce, wine, and pepper and spoon over vegetables. Return to high heat and stir until everything is well heated through and sauce starts to thicken. You want the vegetables to be tender-crisp. Serve immediately.

Each serving provides:

182	Calories	29 g	Carbohydrate
4 g	Protein	288 mg	Sodium
6 g	Total fat	0 mg	Cholesterol

Vegetable-Stuffed Red Peppers

Peppers have come into their own since we discovered just how nutrient-dense they are. Did you know that one green bell pepper is reported to have more vitamin C than a medium-size orange? The red peppers do as well, plus they have beta-carotene.

It is more practical to serve this dish in summer or early fall, when the price of red peppers is reasonable. In winter, you could substitute small acorn squash for the peppers. The proportions will depend on how many you plan to serve. This can be made ahead, refrigerated, then reheated just before serving.

Makes 4 servings

2	large-size red peppers, cut in half and seeded
1	can (7^1/$_2$ ounces) tomato sauce
1	teaspoon fresh dill, snipped
1	large carrot, cut in 16 rounds
1	medium zucchini, cut in 16 slices (see directions for zucchini leaves on page 250)
8	brussels sprouts, cut in half

Steam red pepper halves over boiling water until fork-tender, but don't overcook. Chill under cold running water. Place in a greased shallow baking dish. Mix tomato sauce with dill and spoon a small amount of sauce into bottom of pepper halves.

Steam carrot, zucchini, and brussels sprouts just until tender-crisp. Immediately rinse under cold water to prevent further cooking. Arrange an assortment of vegetables in the red peppers. Vegetables may be refrigerated at this point and placed in the microwave to re-heat just before serving.

Note: Small cubes of squash may be used in place of carrots.

Each serving provides:

64	Calories	15 g	Carbohydrate
3 g	Protein	388 mg	Sodium
1 g	Total fat	0 mg	Cholesterol

Baked Stuffed Potatoes

We used to prepare these potatoes by whipping them with butter, cream, and cheese until creamy, then replacing in their shells. However, the following lowfat potatoes will satisfy.

They also freeze very well (they are a nice thing to have in the freezer for busy days, so make a few extra and freeze). Wrap potatoes individually in foil and place in freezer. To reheat from a frozen state, remove from foil and place in a preheated 450° oven for 20 minutes; then place under the broiler for 5 minutes.

Makes 2 servings

2   baking potatoes
4   tablespoons lowfat cottage cheese (see note)
       chopped green onion, to taste
       salt and freshly ground pepper, to taste

Preheat oven to 400°. Bake potatoes for 1 hour. Remove potatoes and turn on the broiler. Let potatoes cool slightly, then cut in half lengthwise. Spoon out flesh, leaving skin intact. Lightly mix potato flesh with cottage cheese, green onion, salt, and pepper (don't mash the potato—leave it slightly chunky). Spoon the mixture back into the shells.

Place under the broiler for 5 minutes. Serve hot.

Note: Cottage cheeses vary. If the brand you purchased seems a little runny, place it in a sieve to drain before using.

	Each serving provides:		
241	Calories	52 g	Carbohydrate
8 g	Protein	131 mg	Sodium
1 g	Total fat	1 mg	Cholesterol

Mashed Potatoes with Baked Garlic

The roasted garlic has quite a different flavor than raw or even boiled garlic. It has a nutty, almost sweet, flavor, which combines magically with the potatoes. The non-fat sour cream replaces the butter that the original recipe called for. Make lots!

Makes 8 to 10 servings

2	whole heads of garlic
1/2	teaspoon olive oil
8	medium potatoes, peeled and cut into chunks
3/4	cup lowfat milk
4	tablespoons non-fat sour cream
	salt and pepper, to taste
1/2	cup green onions or chives

Remove outer skin from garlic, leaving head intact. Rub with olive oil. Cover with foil and bake in a 325° oven for 1 to 1 1/2 hours. Cool and squeeze out garlic; reserve. Boil potatoes; drain and mash with milk, sour cream, salt, and pepper. Add garlic and green onions or chives. Serve hot.

Note: If you have no time to bake the garlic, add 1 or 2 cloves of fresh garlic to the potatoes when cooking, drain, then mash together when cooked.

Each serving provides:

203	Calories	45 g	Carbohydrate
5 g	Protein	30 mg	Sodium
1 g	Total fat	1 mg	Cholesterol

Hurry-Up Mashed Potatoes

Many of the beef recipes in this book are best complemented with mashed pota-
toes. Sometimes when you are pressed for time, this recipe will be invaluable.

Makes 4 servings

4   serving-size instant mashed potato flakes
1   tablespoon dried onions, put in water to
        be used for potato flakes
1   cup cottage cheese, pureed in blender or food processor
1¹/2   teaspoons butter or margarine
        salt and pepper, to taste
1   teaspoon (more or less) paprika

Preheat oven to 350°. Prepare potatoes according to the directions
on the package, but delete the butter and add dried onions to the
water. Fold cottage cheese into the prepared potatoes. Add salt and
pepper to taste. Empty potato mixture into casserole dish and dot top
with butter. Sprinkle paprika over top and bake for 30 minutes.

	Each serving provides:		
113	Calories	15 g	Carbohydrate
8 g	Protein	262 mg	Sodium
2 g	Total fat	7 mg	Cholesterol

Hash Brown Potatoes

These potatoes are lowfat and super. You must have a cast-iron frying pan or a nonstick pan with a heavy bottom, or this recipe will be an exercise in frustration instead of a delightful and different way of serving potatoes. We usually try to avoid giving recipes whose ingredients are a little ambiguous, but just experiment a bit until you come up with the taste that best suits you. (This is a little reminiscent of recipes handed down from generation to generation, calling for butter the size of an egg or a walnut, or a teacup full of flour—or worse, to add enough flour until it feels right!)

Makes 4 servings

4   potatoes
4   teaspoons minced onion
     salt and pepper, to taste

Peel and grate the potatoes. Squeeze out as much liquid as possible, by hand. Add minced onion, salt, and pepper to taste.

Spray pan well with nonstick cooking spray and press potatoes evenly into pan so that they are fairly compact. Cover and cook over medium-low heat until bottom is nicely browned. This will take about 30 minutes. With a wide spatula, slide potatoes onto flat plate in one piece. Spray pan well again. Return potatoes to pan, and brown uncooked side, uncovered, another 20 to 30 minutes. Don't be tempted to rush the browning process or it will burn, but have heat high enough to cook the potatoes.

You end up with what looks like a large potato cake, about 1 inch thick, which is golden brown and crispy on both sides and soft in the middle. Cut into wedges and serve.

Note: An 8- or 9-inch cast-iron skillet is the right size for 2 very large or 3 medium potatoes.

Each serving provides:			
117	Calories	27 g	Carbohydrate
2 g	Protein	7 mg	Sodium
0 g	Total fat	0 mg	Cholesterol

Lowfat Roast Potatoes

The secret is to partially cook the potatoes by parboiling before they are placed in the oven. If you are a parsnip lover, try this method with parsnips as well, but don't parboil.

Makes 4 servings

4   small to medium potatoes
4   or 8 drops olive oil per potato
       paprika, to taste
       freshly ground black pepper, to taste

Preheat oven to 350°. Peel potatoes, and cut the large ones in half. Cook potatoes in lightly salted boiling water for about 5 minutes. Drain. Let potatoes cool until they are comfortable to handle. Place one or two drops of olive oil in your hands and rub all over each potato. Spray a shallow metal baking pan with nonstick cooking spray. Place potatoes in the pan. Sprinkle with paprika and black pepper, then spray again with nonstick cooking spray. Bake for 30 minutes. Turn potatoes over, spray again, and sprinkle with paprika and pepper. Bake for an additional 30 minutes or until golden brown and tender when pierced with a two-tined fork.

Each serving provides:

128	Calories	27 g	Carbohydrate
2 g	Protein	7 mg	Sodium
1 g	Total fat	0 mg	Cholesterol

Potato and Turnip Casserole

This is an excellent vegetable dish to serve with roasts. It's also good with meat loaf.

Makes 6 to 8 servings

3	cups diced potatoes
3	cups diced yellow turnips
1	tablespoon butter
1	tablespoon flour
1	teaspoon chicken bouillon mix
1	cup 2 percent evaporated canned milk
1/4	teaspoon salt
	pinch of white pepper
	pinch of nutmeg

Preheat oven to 350°. Cook potatoes and turnips together in a large saucepan full of boiling water until tender, about 20 minutes. Drain. Lightly spray a casserole dish with nonstick cooking spray. Place potatoes and turnips in the casserole.

To make the lowfat cream sauce, melt butter in small saucepan. Stir in flour and bouillon mix. Gradually stir in evaporated milk, salt, pepper, and nutmeg. Cook over medium heat, stirring constantly, until sauce thickens, 3 to 5 minutes. Pour sauce over vegetables and bake until hot and bubbly, 20 to 30 minutes.

Each serving provides:			
103	Calories	17 g	Carbohydrate
4 g	Protein	303 mg	Sodium
2 g	Total fat	9 mg	Cholesterol

Baked Cherry Tomatoes

No-fat and colorful. You must peel the tomatoes, so you wouldn't want to make these for a large crowd. Pour boiling water over tomatoes for a few seconds and the skins will slip off easily.

Makes 4 servings

1   pint cherry tomatoes (small basket)
       juice of 1/2 lemon
       several dashes Tabasco
       salt and pepper, to taste
1/2   onion, finely chopped
       chopped fresh parsley or chives

Preheat oven to 350°. Peel cherry tomatoes and place in a baking dish. Mix together the lemon juice, Tabasco, salt, and pepper and pour over tomatoes. Sprinkle the chopped onion and parsley on top and bake, covered, until just heated through, 10 to 15 minutes.

Each serving provides:

26	Calories	6 g	Carbohydrate
1 g	Protein	6 mg	Sodium
0 g	Total fat	0 mg	Cholesterol

Tomatoes with Chopped Mushroom Filling

This is great with steaks or roasts.

Makes 6 servings

6	medium, firm tomatoes
1¹/₂	tablespoons butter or margarine
3	cups chopped fresh mushrooms
¹/₂	cup dry whole wheat bread crumbs
1	large egg, well beaten
1	tablespoon chopped parsley
2	tablespoons chopped chives
¹/₂	teaspoon salt
¹/₄	teaspoon black pepper
1	teaspoon curry powder, scant
	pinch of dry mustard

Preheat oven to 375°. Wash tomatoes, cut top ¹/₄ inch from top and carefully scoop out their insides, leaving hollow shells. Place upside down on a double thickness of paper towels to drain.

In a medium-sized skillet melt the butter and sauté the chopped mushrooms until tender. Stir in the bread crumbs and cool slightly. Add the egg, parsley, chives, salt, pepper, curry powder, and dry mustard. Mix well and fill the tomato shells with this mixture.

Spray a glass pie plate with nonstick cooking spray. Place tomatoes on the plate and bake for 15 to 20 minutes. The tomatoes should retain their shape and the filling should be heated through.

Each serving provides:

86	Calories	10 g	Carbohydrate
3 g	Protein	256 mg	Sodium
5 g	Total fat	44 mg	Cholesterol

Broiled Zucchini

*If you prefer to bake these, place in a preheated 350° oven for 20 to 30
minutes, or until fork-tender.*

Makes 4 servings

2	young zucchini, 6 to 7 inches in length
2	teaspoons olive oil
	salt and pepper, to taste
1¹/₂	tablespoons freshly grated Parmesan cheese

Preheat broiler. Cut zucchini in half lengthwise and score the cut
side with a sharp knife. Brush the cut surface lightly with olive oil and
sprinkle with salt, pepper, and Parmesan cheese. Place under broiler
for 10 minutes.

Each serving provides:

42	Calories	3 g	Carbohydrate
2 g	Protein	38 mg	Sodium
3 g	Total fat	2 mg	Cholesterol

Grated Zucchini au Gratin

You can adjust the amount of zucchini to accommodate the number of servings—make it for two or twelve!

Makes 4 to 6 servings

2	medium zucchini (4 ounces each), coarsely grated (leave skin on)
2	teaspoons grated onion
	salt and pepper, to taste
2	to 3 teaspoons freshly grated Parmesan cheese

Preheat broiler. Spray a nonstick skillet with nonstick cooking spray. Season grated zucchini with the onion, salt, and pepper. Sauté lightly, just until it begins to soften. Remove from heat and empty into shallow casserole dish. Sprinkle with the grated Parmesan cheese and place under the broiler until the cheese is brown.

Each serving provides:

13	Calories	1 g	Carbohydrate
1 g	Protein	32 mg	Sodium
1 g	Total fat	1 mg	Cholesterol

Zucchini Leaves

For a special dinner party, this dish will dress up the dinner plate nicely.

Makes 4 servings

2   medium zucchini

Cut strips from unpeeled zucchini. With a sharp knife, shape into leaves and score for veins. Blanche (plunge into boiling water for 2 minutes, then into ice water). At serving time, heat in the microwave for 3 to 4 minutes. Arrange leaves on a dinner plate.

Each serving provides:

5	Calories	1 g	Carbohydrate
0 g	Protein	1 mg	Sodium
0 g	Total fat	0 mg	Cholesterol

Doreen's Special Salad

We had to include this salad, because it goes perfectly with the curry recipes in this book.

Makes 4 servings

1	head butter lettuce
1/2	cup thinly sliced purple onion (or any sweet onion)
1/2	red pepper, sliced
1	can (10 ounces) mandarin oranges, drained
1/2	cup banana chips
1/3	cup raisins
1/2	teaspoon poppy seeds, optional
1/4	to 1/3 cup bottled Italian-style salad dressing (see note)

Wash, dry, and tear lettuce into bite-sized pieces and place in a salad bowl. Add onion, red pepper, mandarin oranges, banana chips, and raisins.

Add optional poppy seeds to salad dressing, shake well, and drizzle dressing over salad. Toss and serve.

Note: Kraft Zesty Italian dressing is made with canola oil, and Doreen swears it is the best dressing for this particular salad (and you just don't argue with Doreen!).

Each serving provides:

231	Calories	33 g	Carbohydrate
2 g	Protein	125 mg	Sodium
12 g	Total fat	0 mg	Cholesterol

Caesar Salad

*Steak houses around the country would have a hard time keeping their clien-
tele if they didn't have a good Caesar salad on the menu, right? These two
foods have developed a natural affinity. Because we have many good steaks in
this book, a reduced-fat version of this famous salad seemed a must. We ex-
perimented with several dressings to get a true Caesar flavor and yet fewer
grams of fat. The following version was a great success. You must follow the
recipe for the dressing exactly.*

*To make Caesar salad, you must use romaine lettuce—preferably the
inner two-thirds (save the outer leaves for another use). The fish sauce is also
an important ingredient and can be found in the Asian food section of your
supermarket or at specialty grocers. It comes in quite a large bottle, but it is
inexpensive and keeps very well in the refrigerator.*

The secret to the lowfat croutons is to have a good mister (spray bottle).

Makes 4 servings

Lowfat Croutons
1	slice bread
1/2	teaspoon garlic powder
1/2	teaspoon Parmesan cheese

Salad
1	head romaine lettuce
2	tablespoons canola oil
2	tablespoons red wine vinegar
2	tablespoons soy sauce
2	cloves garlic, minced
1	whole egg (see note)
	pinch of dry mustard
1/8	teaspoon fish sauce

To make the croutons, preheat oven to 300°. Place bread on a
cookie sheet and mist lightly with water. Sprinkle with garlic powder
and Parmesan cheese on both sides. You don't want to soak the
bread, just have it moist enough so the garlic powder and Parmesan
cheese will adhere. Bake for 12 minutes. Turn the bread over with a
spatula and bake an additional 10 minutes. Remove from the oven
and immediately cut into cubes. Makes 1 cup croutons.

Wash lettuce, dry, and chill well (you can't make a good Caesar
salad with limp lettuce). Tear lettuce into a salad bowl.

To make the dressing, place oil, vinegar, soy sauce, garlic, egg, dry mustard, and fish sauce in a blender and mix well. Toss salad with enough dressing to moisten. Add 1/2 to 1 cup croutons and toss again. Serve at once, with a bowl of freshly grated Parmesan or shredded Asiago cheese to guests whose diet is not too restricted.

Note: If you are reluctant to use an uncooked egg, substitute 2 tablespoons of lite mayonnaise for the egg. If you do this, reduce soy sauce to 1 tablespoon plus 2 teaspoons.

Each serving provides:			
115	Calories	6 g	Carbohydrate
4 g	Protein	630 mg	Sodium
9 g	Total fat	53 mg	Cholesterol

Spinach Salad

Right behind Caesar salad in popularity is spinach salad. Our scaled-down-in-fat dressings are perfect with tender young spinach leaves.

Makes 4 servings

Salad
$1/2$ pound fresh spinach
4   large fresh mushrooms
$1/2$ can water chestnuts, drained and sliced
$1/4$ medium red or other mild onion, thinly sliced, optional
2   hard-cooked eggs, white only, diced

Orange-Sesame Dressing
$1/4$ cup olive oil
$1/2$ teaspoon sesame oil
$1/4$ cup red wine vinegar
$1/4$ cup orange juice
1   teaspoon soy sauce
$1/2$ teaspoon black pepper
2   teaspoons prepared mustard
$1/4$ teaspoon sugar

Chutney Dressing
3   tablespoons canola oil or safflower oil
3   tablespoons red wine vinegar
3   tablespoons Major Grey's Chutney
        (finely chop any large pieces)
$1/8$ teaspoon garlic powder
$1 1/2$ teaspoons Dijon mustard
$1/8$ teaspoon sugar

Trim off and discard any tough stems or bruised spinach leaves. Wash well in cold water. Shake off excess water and wrap in paper towels. Store in refrigerator to chill well, about 1 hour.

Place dressing ingredients in a small jar and shake well.

When ready to serve, tear spinach into salad bowl. Add mushrooms, water chestnuts, and optional onion slices. Toss with dressing and sprinkle diced egg white over top.

Orange-Sesame Dressing

Each serving provides:

175	Calories	9 g	Carbohydrate
4 g	Protein	156 mg	Sodium
15 g	Total fat	0 mg	Cholesterol

Chutney Dressing

Each serving provides:

167	Calories	15 g	Carbohydrate
4 g	Protein	145 mg	Sodium
11 g	Total fat	0 mg	Cholesterol

Horseradish Mold

This is much like a tomato aspic. It's a wonderful accompaniment to beef dishes.

Makes 6 to 8 servings

2   cups V-8 juice or tomato-vegetable juice
1   package (3 ounces) strawberry-flavored gelatin
1/4   cup prepared horseradish, or to taste (see note)

Heat V-8 juice in a saucepan to just boiling. Remove from heat and stir in gelatin until completely dissolved. Stir in horseradish, mixing well.

Spray a 4-cup mold with nonstick cooking spray. Empty mixture into mold. Chill until firm, roughly 3 to 4 hours.

For a buffet, choose a ring mold; when serving, fill the center with creamed horseradish.

Note: Taste the mixture when adding horseradish, as it varies in strength from brand to brand. We found 1/4 cup to be the right amount for our taste.

Each serving provides:

61	Calories	14 g	Carbohydrate
1 g	Protein	263 mg	Sodium
0 g	Total fat	0 mg	Cholesterol

Overnight Sweet Onion Salad

You must use sweet onions for this salad, such as Walla Walla, Vidalia, or Maui. The salad is great with beef and will keep for 3 to 4 days in the refrigerator. See the variation below, which is a huge hit at buffets (in the variation, the onions must marinate overnight as opposed to just 1 hour).

Makes 10 to 12 servings

3	large sweet onions, peeled and thinly sliced
1	cup white vinegar
1/2	cup sugar
1	teaspoon salt
1	tablespoon chopped fresh parsley
1	teaspoon dried basil
	pinch of cayenne pepper

Place onions in a container. Combine vinegar, sugar, 1/2 cup water, salt, parsley, basil, and cayenne pepper and stir until sugar is dissolved. Pour over onions and let marinate for at least 1 hour before serving.

Variation

Overnight Sweet Onion Salad: Delete water, salt, parsley, basil, and cayenne pepper from the above recipe and marinate onions in just the vinegar and sugar (be sure to dissolve the sugar in the vinegar before adding onions). Leave overnight. The next day, drain onions very well and mix 1 teaspoon celery seed into 1/2 cup lowfat mayonnaise, then toss with the onions and chill before serving.

Each serving provides:			
57	Calories	14 g	Carbohydrate
1 g	Protein	177 mg	Sodium
0 g	Total fat	0 mg	Cholesterol

Marinated Vegetables in Tomato Baskets

A colorful and nutrient-dense vegetable dish to serve at a summer barbecue.
Try it with one of our flank steaks or a perfectly grilled filet.

Makes 6 servings

6	medium tomatoes
1	to 2 cups broccoli florets
1	to 2 cups cauliflower florets
	pinch of sugar
1	tablespoon chopped chives
1/2	cup bottled lowfat Italian-style salad dressing

Slice off the top one-third of the tomatoes. Hollow out the tomatoes and turn upside down on paper towels to drain.

Blanch the florets by dropping into rapidly boiling water to which a pinch of sugar has been added. When the water returns to the boil, remove from heat and drain. Plunge the florets into ice cold water, drain, and let stand until well cooled. Toss with chives in your favorite lowfat Italian-style salad dressing and let stand for at least 1 hour before serving.

Fill the tomato baskets with the marinated vegetables.

Each serving provides:

55	Calories	8 g	Carbohydrate
2 g	Protein	174 mg	Sodium
3 g	Total fat	1 mg	Cholesterol

Fresh Tomato Salsa

Salsa, not too long ago, was considered a new food item. It is now almost a staple in many kitchens. We all want healthy food that tastes great, so we have to replace the flavor lost by removing or reducing the fat in our diets. Salsa serves us well for this purpose. We have used it in several recipes in this book.

Makes 1 quart

3	large tomatoes, seeded, drained, and chopped fine
4	large green onions, including tops, chopped
1	can (4 ounces) whole green chilies, drained, seeded, and chopped
1	tablespoon olive oil
1	tablespoon plus 1 teaspoon red wine vinegar
3/4	teaspoon salt
1/4	teaspoon cumin
1/4	teaspoon oregano
1/4	teaspoon garlic powder
1	large jalapeño pepper, chopped (about 1 tablespoon)
2	tablespoons chopped fresh cilantro leaves, optional

Combine tomatoes, green onions, and chilies in a medium-size mixing bowl. Add the olive oil, vinegar, salt, spices, and jalapeño. Stir to blend.

Let stand 30 minutes. The salsa may be made 4 hours in advance, covered, and chilled. Add the optional cilantro at serving time.

Note: The cilantro is optional, but if you enjoy the flavor, it is terrific in this particular salsa. The jalapeño peppers used in this recipe are the hot ones!

Two tablespoons provide:

10	Calories	1 g	Carbohydrate
0 g	Protein	56 mg	Sodium
1 g	Total fat	0 mg	Cholesterol

No-Salt Seasoning

This recipe appears in the Lowfat Gourmet Chicken *cookbook. We find it preferable to over-the-counter brands and cheaper. Make extra and give it to friends who are on a salt-restricted diet!*

Makes 1 cup

4	tablespoons dry mustard
4	tablespoons onion powder
2	tablespoons white pepper
1	tablespoon plus 1 teaspoon garlic powder
2	tablespoons paprika
2	tablespoons thyme (ground or powdered)
1	teaspoon basil (ground or powdered)

Stir all of the above ingredients together until well mixed. Store in a glass jar and use as needed. This keeps indefinitely.

Each teaspoon provides:

7	Calories	1 g	Carbohydrate
0 g	Protein	1 mg	Sodium
0 g	Total fat	0 mg	Cholesterol

Browned Flour

This recipe appears in the Lowfat Gourmet Chicken *cookbook, but it is equally important for beef dishes. When you get used to having a jar of browned flour handy, you will not want to be without it. This flour doesn't lump and gives a rich color and good flavor to sauces and gravies. A cast-iron frying pan is best for browning the flour.*

2 cups all-purpose flour

Place 2 cups of flour in a large, heavy-bottom skillet. Stir the flour over low heat with a large cooking spoon. Keep stirring and scraping the bottom of the skillet so the flour does not stick. In a fairly short time, the flour will begin to brown. Stir a little faster at this point, so the flour does not burn. You want it a beige-brown color. Do not let it become too dark, because it will get even darker when added to your sauces and gravies. Don't be tempted to turn the heat up if it seems to be slow in browning, because once it gets started, it browns very quickly.

Store in a jar on kitchen shelf. It will last indefinitely. Use in place of any white flour called for in sauces or gravies. It has its own distinctive flavor and is widely used by chefs throughout Europe.

	One-quarter cup provides:		
100	Calories	22 g	Carbohydrate
4 g	Protein	0 mg	Sodium
0 g	Total fat	0 mg	Cholesterol

B. J.'s No-Fat Bread for Bread-Making Machines

*Bread-making machines are becoming increasingly popular, for two reasons:
it is more economical to make your own, and people like to know exactly what
they are eating. (When we served this to our husbands at the last book-testing
and told them there was absolutely no fat in this bread, they both said
"Great!"—and immediately put extra butter on their portions!) There are
so many good stews and pot roasts in this book that we thought a recipe
for a good sopping-up bread would be appreciated.*

*This recipe is for a large loaf, so be sure your bread-making machine
accommodates a large-size loaf. Warning: This bread is very addictive!*

Makes 1 loaf (16 slices)

2	teaspoons sugar
1^1/$_2$	teaspoons salt
3	cups flour
2	teaspoons RAPIDMIX or Fleischmann's Quick Rise yeast

Put 1^1/$_2$ cups water, sugar, salt, flour, and yeast into the bread-
making container in order given and process.

Each slice provides:

97	Calories	20 g	Carbohydrate
3 g	Protein	201 mg	Sodium
0 g	Total fat	0 mg	Cholesterol

Tomato Chutney

This is a delicious condiment to serve with beef and a must *if you serve the Tourtière (page 184).*

Makes 5 pints

3	pounds tomatoes, sliced
2	large apples, chopped
1	medium onion, chopped
1	lime, very finely chopped or shredded in food processor
1/4	pound dates, chopped
1/2	pound raisins
11/2	pounds sugar
1/2	teaspoon cinnamon
1/2	teaspoon ground cloves
1/2	teaspoon allspice
1	tablespoon salt
2	cups vinegar

Place all ingredients in a Dutch oven or large pot and stir to mix well. Cook, uncovered, at a slow boil over medium heat until thick. Mixture will take about 11/2 hours to thicken to the proper consistency. Ladle into sterilized jars and seal.

	Two tablespoons provide:		
49	Calories	13 g	Carbohydrate
0 g	Protein	82 mg	Sodium
0 g	Total fat	0 mg	Cholesterol

Index